party ! food

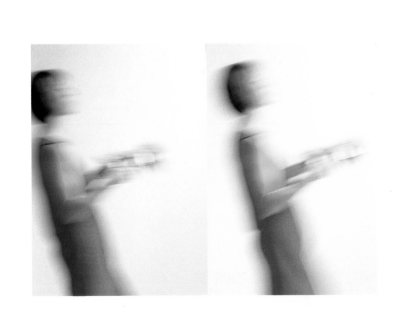

party! food

Lorna Wing

SOMA
san francisco

To my mother, Lottie, and my father, Richard, with my love

First published in 1998 by Conran Octopus Limited.
North American Edition published 1998 by SOMA
Books, by arrangement with Conran Octopus Ltd.
SOMA Books is an imprint of Bay Books & Tapes, Inc.
For information, write: Bay Books & Tapes,
555 De Haro St., No. 220, San Francisco, CA 94107.

ISBN 1-57959-040-3. Library of Congress
Cataloging-in-Publication Data on file with publisher.

For the UK edition:
Commissioning Editor: Suzannah Gough
Consultant Cookery Editor: Jenni Muir
Proofreader/Indexer: Keith Davidson
Americanization: Norma MacMillan
Art Director: Leslie Harrington
Art Editor: Mary Staples
Photographer: Jan Baldwin
Home Economist: Lindsey Greensted-Benech
Stylist: Sue Parker
Production: Suzanne Sharpless

For the SOMA edition:
Publisher: James Connolly
Editorial Director: Clancy Drake
Art Director: Jeffrey O'Rourke
North American Editor: Carolyn Miller
Cover Design: Level Design
Production: Patrick David Barber

Distributed by Publishers Group West
Printed in China
10 9 8 7 6 5 4 3 2 1

contents

Lorna understands how to make a party memorable, for all the right reasons. She combines meticulous planning and stalwart reliability with tasty food and a creative eye. I first met Lorna in the early eighties, when she was doing the food for the party after one of my son Jasper's fashion shows. One of the things that caught everyone's fancy was the mini-portions of fish and chips served in cones made from the *Financial Times* newspaper, a nice, quirky juxtaposition that has since been imitated by many people. But Lorna got there first.

The other thing that impressed me about Lorna was her quiet efficiency. Not surprisingly, she very quickly acquired an excellent reputation and an enviable list of clients. When, in 1986, we bought the Heal's furniture store on London's Tottenham Court Road, we completely overhauled the shop and introduced a scheme that incorporated a new restaurant. Although she took some convincing, Lorna finally accepted the job of running the restaurant and, for the next five years or so, made a great job of it at the same time as building her catering business.

She succeeded at both because she knows there is nothing worse than bland, soggy, unimaginative food that ends up being hidden in the pots and killing the plants.

Lorna's recipes are colorful, innovative, and inspiring, but above all, delicious. How could your guests fail to be impressed by dishes like Brioches Filled with Scrambled Eggs & Caviar, or Raspberry & Lemon Syllabub Trifle?

As a lover of good wines, I get irritated when completely inappropriate wines are served, and even then, incorrectly. Lorna knows precisely what wine to have for the occasion and how much will be needed. (What a disaster if you run out halfway through the party!) She can put together a fantastic selection of cocktails and never fails to astound me with such innovative drinks as Oyster Shooters or Chocolate Martinis. Seductive as they are, it's probably not a good idea to try them all in the same evening.

As much as I enjoy cooking for my family and friends, I hate having to work to a time limit. Lorna has the priceless ability to take the stress out of the organization of a party. Seemingly nothing goes wrong at her events and everything runs to plan. She always gives the impression that she is having as much fun as everyone else.

What greater praise can there be?

Terence Conran

Holding parties is a wonderful excuse to gather

together family and friends in a relaxed environment, to ply them with interesting food and wine, to have stimulating conversation, and above all, to have a great time. In the past twenty years I've probably organized five thousand or so parties: small ones, large ones, glamorous ones, and cozy ones, for the rich and famous, and for those who are neither. Some have tiny budgets, while others spare no expense. But they all have to work — you don't get a second chance on someone's special day. Of course I've had my disasters and learned from them. There was the occasion when I inadvertently set off the fire alarm while glazing a sugary pudding and eighteen burly firemen turned up unannounced to join in the party. And then there was the time when all the power failed during a dinner for five hundred. After such episodes, I quickly learned that the most important thing to do was to plan, double-check, check some more, and to take nothing for granted. This book combines the experience of many years spent earning my living from the party business. It has all you need to know about holding a successful party and how to prepare the food and drinks that will make it memorable. **Enjoy.**

The more planning you can do for a party (apart from impromptu occasions) the better you will enjoy it. Who wants to be slaving away over a hot stove when everyone else is having fun? That is not the point of a party. It is for all concerned to have a good time, and that includes the cook. This section shows how, with a little forethought and list making, you can make sure your party runs smoothly — and that the result is the kind of event you really want to hold. First of all, ask yourself the five essential questions: why, when, where, who, and what.

planning

The answers will help you decide the type of party you want to hold. Each decision will have an impact on another. For example, the space you have available will affect the number of people you can invite. You may decide that it is impossible to fit in the numbers you had hoped for but that you are not prepared to ask fewer people. So, an alternative location might need to be found. This could mean hiring a venue requiring you to use one of their approved caterers, which in turn would bring its own set of restrictions. Ultimately, all these decisions will help you to determine another crucial factor: your budget.

Budgeting

Different parties need different budgets, so think carefully about the type of party you want to hold, as they have differing cost implications. The many variables will have an impact on how you end up spending your money.

Generally, the least expensive way to entertain is to have a cocktail party; at the other end of the scale, a seated meal for lots of people can be extremely costly if it means you will have to rent equipment, pay professional staff to help you, and so on. If you do have to rent equipment from specialty companies, a substantial amount of your budget can be easily swallowed up — if you are able to borrow from family and friends, so much the better. Glasses and bar equipment for cocktail parties are usually quite reasonable to rent, whereas renting tables, chairs, linen, tableware, and mobile kitchen equipment can take up a hefty chunk of your budget.

When planning a small cocktail party or a meal at home where you are serving wines and soft drinks, you will need to spend about equal amounts of money on food and drinks. However, if you are going to serve particularly expensive champagne, wines, or foods, that ratio will obviously alter. If you need to keep your costs down, it is best not to offer too much choice of food or drinks.

You need to establish your own priorities and decide where you wish to allocate your budget. For some people, the food served is far more important than the drinks, and for others, the entertainment will take greater priority. To each his own.

Menu

Only once you know how many people you can invite, can you start planning your menu. Think about the kind of people you are inviting to your party, and why. Are they young or old? Do they tend to have hearty appetites, or tiny ones because every calorie is being counted? Are there any specific dietary, religious, or medical needs the menu must account for? Or are your guests just plain fussy?

The recipes in this book are arranged into three main sections. Food you can eat in the hand, food you need to eat with a fork, and drinks, alcoholic and nonalcoholic. Choose what suits your personal lifestyle the best. There will be occasions when you want to pull out all the stops and others when you cannot summon up the energy to cook a single thing — that is fine. I am including recipes that can be done well ahead of time and require little or no cooking, as well as recipes that are a bit more complicated. There are dishes for the new and inexperienced cook and for those who know their way around the kitchen. Most recipes are for ten, but you can easily divide or multiply them to suit your needs.

However, it is important to remember that, in the end, it is only food and there is always a solution if disaster strikes. It might be calling the local fish and chips shop and arranging to collect fifty portions of their best. Serve them, still wrapped in newspaper, with that vintage champagne you had been planning to drink. Or boil up all the pasta you can lay your hands on and serve it with four store-bought sauces. Your guests are there to enjoy themselves in your company; watching you panic about a culinary disaster will only make them uncomfortable.

Is Sunday morning the only time you have to ask people over? Great. Brunches typify the new style of entertaining, where guests are happy to sit perched on a bar stool quaffing drinks and will happily give the cook a hand with the preparation.

The event

So, what type of event is it to be? Are you celebrating a special, once-in-a-lifetime family occasion such as a wedding or christening? Perhaps Sunday morning is the only time you can spare to have people over. Or, there could be no particular reason to celebrate and you simply want to get together with some fun friends, enjoy a few cocktails, and nibble on some snacks.

Fortunately, the rules have now changed about how we entertain at home. Gone are the days of the stuffy three-course meal, invariably eaten in the dining room on the "best" china.

Nowadays, we are just as likely to be perched on a stool in the kitchen, quaffing wine and giving the cook a hand in between courses. It is your party, so do what suits you and your lifestyle.

Breakfasts & brunches

Weekends are for brunch and for friends meandering over, newspapers in hand, as and when it suits them. It is flextime, anywhere between late morning and early afternoon, but never before midday if you have any sense. For me, brunches are the best. It is a time when you can ask friends over knowing that they will not stay as long as an invitation to lunch would

signal. It then leaves the rest of the day to kick off your shoes, catch up on the papers and finish off the rest of the bubbly. Breakfasts and brunches worth getting up for are anything with smoked salmon, waffles and bagels, and eggs every possible way. And, of course, copious and reviving quantities of coffee.

For those who want an effortless AM start, this book has ideas for no-cook, buy-absolutely-everything menus to make brunches as painless as possible. And for those who find cooking pleasurable, I am giving lots of hearty one-pot dishes, like my Butter Chicken Masala. A glass of steaming hot frothy chocolate with churros makes a decadent finish to any brunch. Roll on next Sunday!

Lunch & suppers

Lunch can be pizza. Lunch can be pasta. In fact, lunch can be anything you want it to be. Most of all, it should be spontaneous and uncomplicated. Ditto supper. Make it effortless, with as much as possible of the preparation and cooking done way ahead of time.

For these rather informal occasions, try a mixture of finger and fork foods. In warm weather, nibble on some vegetable-based canapés for an appetizer or first course. Follow with an all-in-one salad.

In cold months, make a big cauldron of jambalaya or cheesy polenta, the kind of hearty, sustaining dishes that are enough to rid anyone of the winter blues. Do not ignore sandwiches when you are entertaining informally — they do not have to be the curled-up cheese and

Picnic food must be portable and sturdy enough to withstand the journey. Hand-held food is the most convenient. A collection of savory pastries is good to snack on during a day at the beach or in the country and can be easily transported in a box.

tomato variety. What about a sizzlingly hot soft-shelled crab sandwich? Or, the ultimate in chic, a caviar sandwich? At the other end of the scale, you could try a Sloppy Joe of hot and spicy chili piled into pita bread, great for those times when you have friends over to down a few beers and to watch a game on television. Side orders, such as my hot Garlic Potato Chips and Sweet Potato Fries, make sandwiches into more of an occasion yet are popular with most people.

Picnics & barbecues

Picnics, even if they are only in the garden, must be portable. You have to be able to carry them without the assistance of a sherpa. So, do not be tempted to take along breakable and weighty tableware — leave it all at home for other, more appropriate, occasions. If you are embarking on a journey, the food has to be well chosen to survive the sweltering heat of a car trunk or being carried on your back in a backpack. Picnics can run

the entire gamut from grandiose and grown-up occasions to straightforward and simple. But if you are wise, you will decide on the latter. Good eat-in-the-hand foods are often pastry based, such as a goat cheese and zucchini pastry, or wrapped items, like my Lettuce-Wrapped Moroccan Meatballs. The same can be said for chunky sandwiches — great for picnics.

Do not forget about winter picnics; they have their own appeal. Wrap yourself up warmly against the elements and serve something sustaining and hot, like a fruity lamb tagine or red duck curry from a wide-necked thermos.

Barbecues are the delight of many a cook. They are a great excuse to be freed from the confines of the indoor kitchen and to relinquish the culinary duties to someone else. Keep barbecues simple. Do not be tempted, for one single moment, to make them sophisticated.

Outdoor entertaining makes for heartier appetites and requires robust foods, so supplement the sausages and burgers with sticky Thai chicken wings and marinated vegetable skewers. Throw fat, juicy shrimp, still in their shells, onto the grill, along with a rack or two of ribs. Have ice-cold white wine and lots of nonalcoholic concoctions at hand.

And to finish? Try sweet bruschetta topped with the best of the summer's fruits. Peaches, strawberries, raspberries, and a dollop of mascarpone cheese are a divine combination. Cakes and pastries, bite-sized or a generous wedge, are always a treat. If all that seems like too much effort, the lazy cook can always substitute rounds of oozing cheeses and baskets of plump fruits, ripe to the point of bursting.

Afternoon tea

Afternoon tea, traditionally taken at 4 on the dot, is for most of us a relic of the past, so when the opportunity does arise, do it in style! Teatime is an ideal way to enjoy a lazy afternoon with friends and a perfect excuse to indulge in luscious cakes that you would not normally dream of eating. It is also the perfect way to celebrate a christening or wedding.

At such times, the first thing that people want when they arrive is a drink. It could be something innocuous, like my glorious frappé of strawberries and cream, or a glass of Long Island Iced Tea (an innocent name for a lethal cocktail).

After the initial drinks have made the rounds, follow up quickly with the food, as you will find that everyone is ravenous by this time. Never be amazed at people's capacity to eat on these occasions, and always allow more food than you could ever have imagined possible.

Food for tea should be small, or at the most should be capable of being eaten with one hand. Plates are perfectly acceptable for gathering up a little selection of goodies, but forget using forks, except for those sticky cakes.

Cocktail parties

Cocktail parties come in different guises. There are those where guests arrive promptly at the allotted cocktail hour for a glass of champagne and a few exquisite but insubstantial canapés before going on to dinner or home for supper. And then there are those where you know that guests will not be leaving until the wee small hours of the morning. The former is an excellent way of entertaining lots of people in one fell swoop, as it is unlikely that they will all arrive at once. Some

they have a supply of cocktail napkins at the ready for greasy fingers. Pace the food, starting with cold items then moving on to hot. Limit yourself to only one or two that require last-minute attention.

In an ideal world, you would probably have one completely effortless canapé, one canapé with a dip, and a bowl of something like Garlic Potato Chips that people can happily pick at. Then you might have a crisp vegetable canapé, followed by two bread-based items for a bit of substance. A pastry tart, followed by something deep-fried, such as miniature fish and chips, would round it off nicely. Avoid mixing different canapés on a serving plate, as you will create more impact with twenty identical items. It also makes replenishing the dish much faster.

When your cocktail party is going to last for as long as people are having fun, and the food therefore needs to be quite substantial, treat it like a meal and serve it in courses. Start with some small canapés and follow with more filling finger foods, like bruschetta, sandwiches, or pizza. Put out small plates for these. Finally, serve some sweet foods, reverting back to bite-sized items again, such as little summer fruit tartlets.

There is another sort of cocktail occasion that is neither canapés nor substantial finger foods. It is simply friends over for snacks and nibbles, maybe stopping off on their way home from work, or coming over on a Saturday night for a housewarming. You do not always want to start from scratch, so this

guests will stay for half an hour, while others are there for the duration. At these sorts of cocktail parties the food is bite-sized and generally served. For the latter type of party though, you need to treat it as a mini-buffet, giving guests the qualities of a cocktail party combined with the sustenance of a meal.

The great thing about cocktail parties is that the guests can be a mix of

professional and personal acquaintances. Best of all, it allows everyone to circulate freely, moving on quickly if they get stuck with someone they find boring.

For a two-hour cocktail event, you want only bite-sized canapés so that guests don't have to worry about catching crumbs in one hand while balancing a drink in the other. Enlist willing volunteers to help hand out the food, making sure

is when you want to make clever use of store-bought ingredients or foods that can be whipped out of the freezer.

It might be some Sesame Cheese Straws and Anchovy Pastries, which will only take a few minutes to heat up in the oven. Or, it might be a packet of potato chips over which you toss some hot garlic butter before warming through. Herby nuts, spicy olives, and jars of sun-dried tomatoes and marinated artichokes all belong here, with slices of cheese and salami. Gather this collection of foods, put them into bowls, and arrange half a dozen on a tray as a stylish way of making simple foods look good.

As far as drinks are concerned, the sky's the limit. Good champagne or sparkling wines are never spurned, nor are still wines or great make-ahead cocktails. But whatever you decide to serve, make sure that you always have mineral water and soft drinks available. It is important to remember that there are lots of folks who don't drink alcohol, and that at every party there are bound to be designated drivers who still need to be included in the fun. Any decent liquor store will offer plenty of nonalcoholic beers and wines, too.

What I particularly love about cocktail parties is that they are a wonderful opportunity to show off your style. There are myriad serving dishes you can choose from to make your mark. Contemporary steel, glass, and pottery give canapés a modern, sleek look, while wooden plates and baskets lined with grapevine or banana leaves give a natural, earthy feel. Take your pick to match your mood.

Cocktail parties are the best means of entertaining a large number of people and an ideal way to socialize with personal and professional acquaintances. Guests can circulate freely and no one is expected to spend the entire night talking to one person.

Bring your own

Bring your own, or BYO, parties, where everyone brings a bottle to drink, can help keep the costs of throwing a party to a minimum. However, if this is your plan, make sure you allow sufficient drinks of your own for everyone to have at least a glass each before relying on any donated bottles. Do not forget that you will need to chill white wines and beers, so either make room in the fridge or pick up some extra ice and make sure that you get them chilled as soon as possible, as it will take about an hour to get everything to the right temperature.

Another cost-effective way of entertaining is to ask everyone to bring a dish instead of a bottle. But if you plan to do this, remember you still need to organize the menu and be specific about

what you want friends to contribute, as you do not want them all turning up with the same food. This type of party is also a good way of spreading the workload if you know you are going to be frantically busy — and it is much more fun than slaving away in the kitchen on your own.

The location

The space you choose for entertaining depends entirely on the kind of party you are giving, as well as the numbers, the weather, and your budget. So, deciding on the location, at home or elsewhere, indoors or outdoors, is one of the initial hurdles to overcome.

If the party is to be at home, especially if it is for larger numbers, be inventive. Be prepared to clear out furniture. The hallway could become a dining room. A bedroom could become the bar.

When the space inside your home is not suitable for one reason or another, a tent may be the answer. You might just need to extend your house with a canopy tacked on to the patio, or you may require a large free-standing tent to accommodate the whole party. Be guided by the experts on the type and size of structure. Safety is paramount when erecting temporary structures on slopes or different levels, so there needs to be a balance between aesthetics and practicalities.

Tents, these days, are sophisticated and can be beautifully lined in all shades. It might be the simplicity of pure white pleating. Or it might be the effect of a night sky created by lining the marquee entirely in black and lighting it with

Even at parties where guests are asked to bring their own drinks, make sure you are able to offer at least one glass of alcohol per person before relying on any donated bottles.

hundreds of tiny twinkling lights. Do not forget that in cold months you will also need to organize some form of heating.

For large events at home, expect to have your life disrupted for anything up to a week, particularly if tents are being erected and generators need to be brought in. There will also be numerous deliveries from dawn to dusk. Remember, too, that the party is not over when your guests go home. Some contractors will take everything away with them on the day, but others will need to return to dismantle tents, remove bulky equipment, and so on.

If you do decide to hold your party at home, make a realistic appraisal of all the resources you have available. Do not be too ambitious and do not overload your resources. Consider not only your kitchen space, but also your oven, fridge, and freezer capacities. Is there enough room in your kitchen to prepare a hot fork lunch for fifty? Do you have sufficient glasses, china, cutlery, and all the necessary kitchen paraphernalia for that lunch? If not, do you want, or can you afford, to hire it? Or would it make more sense instead to serve a cold finger-food menu, not requiring plates or cutlery? How much time are you likely to have to prepare the food yourself in the days before to the party and on the day itself? Or will you need some help with the cooking and serving? All these decisions will have an impact on the food and drink that you serve.

It is quite possible that you will have to supplement the furniture and equipment you have at home. There are numerous companies that rent tables, chairs, china, glassware, tablecloths, and mobile kitchens, including ovens, fridges, and freezers, from the very mundane to the

Party checklist

I find the best way to approach organizing a party, large or small, is to "walk the course" in my head from start to finish. Think about where guests will park their cars; where a cloakroom needs to be set up for coats; if a receiving line, informal or otherwise, is required; and where the first drinks will be served. Where should the tables and chairs be situated?

Are you going to dance, and if so, is there a suitable dance floor, or will you need to bring one in? What decorations, floral or otherwise, are needed for the tables and room? Consider the best place acoustically for musicians to set up. Is the lighting adequate, or does it need to be supplemented with candles and special lighting? Most important, do you have sufficient power for all of this lighting, cooking, and entertainment? Only then can you start to plan your party properly.

This checklist is a quick reminder of everything you need to remember when organizing a party. Some points only apply to small parties while others are particular to large parties; however, you will find every event runs more smoothly when you adhere to this basic timetable.

In advance

● Decide what type of party you want to hold, whether seated or standing, formal or informal, large or small.
● Determine your budget.
● Compile your guest list.
● Set the date.
● Calculate if you have sufficient space and kitchen facilities (ovens, fridges, freezers, etc.) to hold your party at home, or if you need to rent a venue. If renting, choose and book the venue.
● Contact and get quotes from suppliers, including caterers; and for tents, florists, mobile toilets, musicians, dance floors, lighting, power supplies, and mobile air conditioning or heaters. Have a look at examples of their work.
● Check you have enough tableware, serving dishes, linen, kitchen equipment, etc. If not, find out if there is anyone you can borrow from, or get a quote for renting equipment.
● Send out invitations, or invite guests by telephone, but only once you know you can do what you want, where you want, and within your budget. Keep a record of acceptances and any special dietary needs.
● Choose the menu, using a varied mix of ingredients, textures, colors, balance of flavors and seasonal foods. Try to choose several dishes that can be prepared well in advance of the party, and remember any guests with special dietary needs.
● Choose the drinks.
● Make detailed shopping lists and order food, the celebratory cake, drinks, ice, equipment, music, flowers, decorations, etc., as appropriate. Buy any unperishable items.
● Cook and freeze any dishes that can be prepared in advance.
● Write or get menus and place cards printed.
● Book staff, if needed. Check if they or any other contractors need a meal.
● Warn the neighbors.

Just before or on the day

● Shop for the remaining food and drinks, plus flowers and any other decorations.
● Prepare the food.
● Check that everything you have ordered has been delivered.
● Arrange flowers and any decorations.
● Put out all glasses, plates, linen, serving dishes, etc.
● Chill the drinks and make any cocktails that can be prepared in advance.
● Organize a space for guests to leave coats.
● Organize a space to put any dirty plates and glasses.
● Have trash cans ready for trash.
● Place clean hand towels and soaps in the bathrooms.
● Brief staff or any people helping with the food or drink.

● **Party!**

extremely elaborate. If it does not cost you any extra, get the equipment the day before so that you have time to unpack and check it all. Most firms will charge you to take everything back dirty, but it is worth paying extra for this service as it will save you hours of washing up.

If you decide that the party cannot be at home, one of your first challenges is finding a suitable venue, as so many get booked months in advance. There are many different types of venues available, from museums to community centers, to club houses and historic houses. Look for them in the Yellow Pages, peruse your local papers, or consult venue guides.

Your decision about where to go will depend on availability, numbers, and decor. Many venues have restrictions about what you can and cannot do. Some will accommodate your every need, allowing you to bring in your favorite caterer and florist and let you drink, smoke, and dance to your heart's content. Then there are other venues where there will be restrictions that will determine whether you want to hold your party there after all. Many museums and historic houses have very specific rules about their buildings and how they are used by outsiders. Sometimes you will have to choose the caterer, lighting people, florist, and entertainers from an approved list.

The behind-the-scenes area is as important as what goes on in the front of the house, as it will have a major effect on much of your decision making. If your home, or the rented venue, does not have sufficient kitchen space, is there another suitable area to build a temporary mobile kitchen? I have set up kitchens in barns with resident bats, in basements when dinner was being served three floors up,

To enhance the atmosphere, keep musicians in
the same room as the party. Most will be able to
suggest where they should be positioned for the
best acoustics, and remember that they will need
to take regular breaks from playing.

and in buildings that were still incomplete
and exposed to all the elements. Caterers
are used to being very enterprising when it
comes to finding space for their kitchens!

Remember to locate an area to leave
all the dirty plates, cutlery, and glasses,
as well as empty bottles and trash. If the
bathroom facilities are poor, pretty them
up with your own soaps and hand towels.

The atmosphere

Once you have chosen where the party is
going to be, decide if you are going to
theme it in any way. It does not have to
be overtly themed, or indeed at all, but it
does help to give focus to the flowers,
table decorations, and so on. There is no
need to go over the top and make all the
food match the colors of the room: Food
should be for real, not made to fit a theme.

Remember that creating an exciting,
interesting mood for a party starts at the
front door. First impressions do count and
set the tone for what is happening inside.
Decorate entrances in a style appropriate
to the party, whether with flowers, foliage,
banners, or fabric. When it is dark, create
a magical mood by hanging votive lights
in trees, or make a candlelit walkway with
a row of garden flares.

Scents too can enhance the mood and
hint at what is in store. Use room sprays
or scented oils, burn incense, choose
beautifully perfumed potpourris, or for
weddings, a romantic flutter of scented
fresh petals. In winter, try warm, spicy
fragrances such as cinnamon, nutmeg,
and vanilla; for summertime, you want
fresh citrus, floral, or herbaceous scents.

Music & dancing

The music at a party should be
memorable, but for the right reasons. Not
only should it make an impact, it should
enhance and complement the whole
event. Music can be cleverly used to
theme a party and match the atmosphere
you want to create. There is such an
array of styles to choose from, whether it
is a salsa or jive band, a cocktail pianist,
1930s French café swing jazz, a string
orchestra, or even Elizabethan minstrels.

For parties such as large family
gatherings, where people of all different
ages are attending, there is no quick-fix
formula for choosing the music as taste
is such a personal thing. But what you
do not want to do is alienate anyone by
playing solely one style. If you are

organizing the party music yourself, there
are some good commercially produced,
ready-mixed CDs and party tapes on the
market that cover a broad spectrum of
tastes. Or you could ask each guest to
bring their favorite CD, along with a
bottle, for a real variety of music.

When you are employing professional
musicians or DJs, make sure that you
spend time with them before the party
and tell them your likes and dislikes. Be
very clear about the sort of mood and
atmosphere you want to create, as it takes
great skill and experience to play the right
music at a party and to judge the mood of
the group accurately.

Music does not have to be loud or
deafening to be good, but it does have to
be at the right volume. Try to contain

music in one area so that guests can move away from it if they want some peace and quiet for talking. Be considerate about the noise levels if you are in a residential area and do not want to upset your neighbors.

Most musicians will have an opinion about the ideal place to be positioned in a room for the best acoustics, but all will agree that they want to be in the same room as the party. If you put them in a second room they will be too cut off and you will not only lose the atmosphere but split the party completely. Do not forget that musicians need regular breaks from playing, so you might need to think about having an alternative source of music while they are resting.

Remember that sound systems will need extra outlets and sufficient power, so make sure that you have enough of both. Be sure that all extension cords or cables are securely taped down to prevent any accidents and that they are safely positioned so they cannot get wet.

If you are planning a large party where everyone is going to dance, it is always best to lay a parquet or wooden floor as it is very hard to dance on an uneven surface like matting. And if you are going to the expense of paying for a band, it is false economy not to have a dance floor as well. Small dance floors are the most effective, as they create an intimacy that a large floor can never achieve. Ideally, this dance floor should be centrally positioned in a room with tables and chairs all around to best enjoy the music and create a party atmosphere.

Lighting

Lighting has a crucial part to play in setting the atmosphere for a party. Candlelight hides a multitude of sins and can make the most dingy of places look stunning. Use masses of candles, of every different shape and size, to transform a space. Make sure that they are positioned in safe places away from anything likely to catch on fire such as flowers, fabric, or if outside, dry grass. I never leave candles unattended, or put them at floor level where it is easy for clothing to catch fire. Keep a fire extinguisher at hand if you plan to have lots of burning candles.

Gas lanterns, kerosene lamps, and votive candles are all great for outside lighting, grouped together or singly. Try to ring the changes. For example, during the festive season, put small candles into highly polished red and green apples. Cut a bit from the base so that it sits securely

A colorful collection of candles makes a pretty table decoration as well as an atmospheric form of lighting. Make sure the flames are kept away from anything that may catch fire, and never leave candles unattended in case of an accident.

and then scoop out the center to take the candle. The same can be done with globe artichokes. To extend the life of the candles, pop them into the freezer for a few hours to slow down their burning.

For large or special parties, lighting experts can create magical effects with spotlights, shaded table lamps, and myriad different lighting techniques. They will outline driveways with flaming torchères, put twinkling lights in trees, bathe rooms with a warm glow, spotlight table centerpieces and create drama on dance floors. They will be sensitive to the mood of the party and can even change the lighting during the course of the evening. You may start, for example, with lighting clear enough so that guests can see everything, then move on to subdued, warmer lighting later on.

Flowers & table decorations

When decorating rooms and tables, decide where you want to concentrate your efforts and money. It might be with a single glorious flower arrangement, or tying napkins with frivolous polka-dot or candy-striped ribbons. If flowers are what you want, raid the garden, go to the flower market at the crack of dawn, or involve your favorite florist.

Florists and decorators can bring originality, drama, and ingenuity to a party. They will help you select a theme for the occasion, be it modern or period, simple or elaborate, and offer arrangements that are tropical, scented, or edible. They will be eminently practical in advising you on color schemes, settings, and which blooms to avoid to stay within budget.

Matching flowers and foliage (and vegetables and fruits) to containers is

Professional florists can bring ingenuity and drama to a special party, advising you on the choice of theme and which out-of-season blooms to avoid to help you stay within your budget.

essential and should tie in with your personal style, taste, and surroundings. Choose from stone, glass, wood, pottery, wicker, china, or metal containers.

You do not have to spend a fortune on decorating tables, nor do they always have to be decorated with flowers. I like having edible table arrangements. Little tubs of sprouting mustard and cress, grouped together in a low wooden box, are effective and inexpensive for a spare, minimalist look. Hollowed-out pumpkin and squash, in autumn months, make natural containers for seed heads, berries, and dried flowers and grasses. For an ethnic feel, pile brightly colored spices like turmeric and paprika into pyramid shapes in shallow metal bowls, Indian-style. Do the same with red and green chilies, rice, lentils, or aromatic star anise. Try to develop your own style and do it with a bit of wit and humor. There is nothing to stop you having a goldfish idly swimming around in a clear glass bowl to decorate an Asian buffet table.

Raid cupboards and drawers and use your imagination to see what you have that can be used. Blankets, throws, and sheets can double as tablecloths. Do not hesitate to give each table a different look if necessary, if it means not having to buy or hire table linens. Or borrow from friends. Remember, everything does not have to match. You may decide on a pale and interesting look, with everything in shades of white and cream. Then again, bright, bold, and clashing might be more to your taste. Equally, it could be your

much-used kitchen china and prized but battered family silver, jazzed up with napkins tied with raffia and flowering herbs. Be bold in whatever you do. Cut over-sized leaves from the garden to use as table mats; use shells for salt and pepper. Line plates or bowls with squares of banana leaves for an inexpensive Asian look.

Handwrite menus and put them into picture frames. Or, for a buffet table, write the name of each dish on a gift tag and tie it to a pear sprayed gold and placed alongside the dish. For an Asian theme, write your menu and a few Chinese characters on rice paper, tie with a silky tassel, or secure with bright red sealing

wax. Place cards or menus poked into fortune cookies are fun and original. So are names written in gold or silver pen on large smooth pebbles or glossy green leaves.

Invitations

If you do not want the expense of printing menus and invitations, do your own. Invitations, whether handwritten, faxed, or formally engraved, should state clearly who is doing what, where, and when. Most importantly, tell your guests what the dress code is. Everyone, regardless how much of a partygoer they are, wants to know what to wear. You should also provide a map or instructions if your home or the location is difficult to find.

FINGER-FOOD PARTIES

Waiting staff: One per 20 guests for serving food and drinks. When you have more than 1 waiter, split the duties of serving the food and drink between them.

Bar staff: One per 100 guests when only champagne, wine, water, and soft drinks are being served. Drinks made to order take much more time to make than just opening a bottle of wine and pouring it. So, if you are serving cocktails, or have a full bar, you will need to have a minimum of 2 per 100 guests.

Cooks: One per 50 guests. While a professional chef can usually cope with assembling 400 hot and cold canapés or finger-food items over a 2-hour period, you would need 2 experienced cooks to manage the same quantities. This assumes that there are not too many items needing last-minute attention.

FORK-FOOD PARTIES

Waiting staff: One per 15 guests for serving food and drinks at a stand-up event. When you have more than 1 waiter, split the duties of serving the food and drink between them. For serving food at a seated event, allow 1 waiter per 10, and for serving drinks allow 1 waiter per 20.

Bar staff: see above.

Cooks: One per 20 to 25 guests. This depends on the variety of dishes and whether the food is hot or cold. It also assumes that most of the preparation has been done and all that is needed is the final assembling or reheating.

Hiring caterers and party planners

Some large-scale parties need to be treated almost like a military exercise. This is where caterers and party planners really come into their own, as they can guide you through the potential entertaining minefields. If you have decided to hand over all the planning to a caterer, first insist on a tasting, unless you are already familiar with their food. It is your party, so you want to be assured that your expectations will be met.

In addition, ask to see the table laid if you plan to have a seated meal. Check that you like the style and quality of the chairs, linen, and tableware — it is such an individual thing and what suits one person may not suit another. Ask, too, to have a sample flower arrangement for the table to make sure that, apart from liking it, you are also able to see your guests over the top of it.

Unsure of the musicians? Ideally, go and hear them play before you finally make up your mind, or failing that, ask for a tape of their work so that you can listen to the music at home.

If you are the one overseeing the whole thing, make sure that all your outside contractors are working together. For instance, the tent company will have to plan with the lighting people, caterer, musicians, and florist to ensure that they all have enough space to work in and that the tent will be ready in time to allow the others to do their bit.

If your budget does not run to hiring a professional photographer to record all your party efforts, place some disposable cameras on the tables for guests to snap pictures instead.

Helping hands

Try, if you can, to get some help with serving the food. If you cannot afford to hire a wait staff or cooks, or it simply is not that kind of party, ask friends, family or teenage children to lend a hand, but make sure that you give them specific duties. Brief them well before the party on exactly what you expect them to do, and show them where everything goes. As timing is so important at parties, you will find it highly advantageous to have a schedule that says who is doing what and at what time.

There may be some occasions, such as large parties or special celebrations, when you will definitely need some professional help. The Yellow Pages or local cooking schools are good places to start looking for staff.

At large parties in particular, you will also need somebody to oversee and manage it all, as well as wait staff, bar staff, cooks, washer-uppers, and a strong body to do all the fetching and carrying. If that is the case, the list on the left is a useful guideline about the numbers of staff you will require. They should arrive about 1½ to 2 hours before the party in order to set up bars, chill wines, lay any tables, and finish preparing the food.

Make sure that you designate a private area with a coatrack and hangers for all these people to leave their coats and personal belongings in safety. Determine whose responsibility it is to feed them and also any contractor's crew.

Finally, do not forget that you will probably have to contribute to the cost of their transport home if the party will be finishing late at night.

Cleaning up

The day before a party I always try to get the house sorted so that all I have to think about on the day itself is finishing off the food, opening bottles, and getting myself ready. Moving furniture, cleaning, arranging flowers, and so forth always takes much longer than you expect, so ideally, if you have the space and your lifestyle allows it, do as much as possible a day in advance.

Make space in the closet so that there is somewhere for guests to hang their coats. Move any unnecessary furniture to allow space for everyone to circulate freely. Sort out hand towels for the bathroom, along with a small sewing kit for repairs and a first-aid kit ready for emergencies. So you do not get inundated with requests for the local taxi service, pin up the telephone number by each phone.

Even when the "staff" are friends and family, make sure you give them specific duties to attend to and brief them on the schedule so that everybody knows who is doing what and when. Ask them to arrive about two hours beforehand to help set up.

Sort out all the serving dishes that you want to use, arrange flowers, set up the bar, and put wines in the fridge to chill.

Once all that has been done, make a list of everything there is left to do on the day, along with a loose timing schedule next to each task. Finally, fill a bucket with water ready to plunge gifts of flowers into so you do not have to spend time arranging them in the midst of the party.

Cleaning up after a party really brings you down to earth with a crash. If you can, get some help with the washing up during the party so you are not left with all the chaos later on. If you do not have any help and cannot face all that cleaning up immediately, get organized beforehand. Clear a space, preferably out of sight, so that you can stack all the dirty dishes in neat piles as you go, line up glasses, and put cutlery into a large bowl of soapy water to soak. Then, throw a cloth over the top and forget about it until later. It is best to dispose of empty bottles in card-board boxes rather than plastic bags, so keep a few stacked beside the trash can. Empty any ashtrays before going to bed, open windows to freshen up the house, and clear the air. Then face it all the next day.

The neighbors

Inform neighbors if you are planning a large party where there will be lots of activity with people parking cars, making noise, and coming and going at all hours. Most neighbors are pretty tolerant, unless you are a habitual noisy party giver who keeps them awake until the small hours. Whenever I have a party, I send a note outlining what is happening, with the expected finishing time, and deliver it with a small bunch of flowers or a bottle of wine. It always works wonders.

Equipment checklist

FINGER-FOOD PARTIES

- Tables, occasional tables and any extra tables for the bar, food preparation, or for holding dirty glasses, plates, etc.
- Tablecloths for the tables and bar.
- Cloth napkins for the bar and waiters.
- Cloth or paper napkins for guests.
- Chairs.
- Coatracks and hangers. Provide a ticketing system for large parties.
- Trash cans or large plastic tubs for chilling drinks and also for trash.
- Plastic sheeting for floor of bar area.
- Glasses: champagne, wine, tumblers, cocktail, highballs, liqueur, or brandy.
- Pitchers for juice
- Ice bucket and spoon.
- Drinks trays.
- Corkscrews and bottle openers.
- Blender, shaker, strainer, long-handled spoon, drinks measures.
- Small board, sharp knife, and bowl for fruit for drinks.
- Ashtrays if smoking is allowed.
- Dish towels and hand towels.
- Serving dishes and bowls.
- Kitchen equipment, ovens, heating trays, fryers, fridge, freezer, baking sheets, saucepans, mixing bowls, etc.
- Ice for chilling and putting into drinks.
- Paper napkins, first-aid kit, candles, matches, swizzle sticks, toilet paper, soap, trash bags, plastic bags, paper towels, plastic wrap, foil, and cleaning cloths.

FORK-FOOD PARTIES

- All the above equipment.
- Tables if seating is required.
- Tablecloths if seating is required.
- Dinner plates and forks.
- Dessert plates and spoons or forks.
- Serving spoons and forks.
- Sauce spoons.
- Salt shakers and peppermills.
- Coffee or teacups and saucers.
- Coffee- or teapots.
- Sugar bowls and cream pitchers.
- Kettles and water or coffee urns.

For those people who are undecided about how they want to entertain, I have put together a versatile menu-planning chart to help devise menus for parties, be they small and intimate or large and informal. This at-a-glance guide can help you make up your mind and give you an idea of the type and quantity of food you will need. Use the chart for all types of events: for casual brunches with your nearest and dearest, for that chic cocktail party when you want to impress, or even to advise your caterer if you are not up to organizing a family wedding on your own.

Perhaps it is high summer and you want to ask a dozen friends over. If so, scan the chart. You may decide to invite them for a mixture of finger and fork food, serving some canapés followed by a cold main course, salad, and a dessert. Alternatively, you could skip the meal and serve simple finger food instead. If your usual lifestyle

menu planning

	Finger Food Only		Finger and Fork Food		Fork Food Only	
	SUMMER	**WINTER**	**SUMMER**	**WINTER**	**SUMMER**	**WINTER**
10–20 PEOPLE	6 cold savories *8–12 items each*	4 cold savories 2 hot savories *8–12 items each*	2 cold canapés *3 items each* 1 cold fork dish 1 salad 1 bread 1 cold dessert	2 cold canapés *3 items each* 1 hot fork dish 1 salad 1 bread 1 cold dessert	1 cold fork dish 1 salad 1 bread 1 cold dessert	1 hot fork dish 1 salad 1 bread 1 cold dessert
30–40 PEOPLE	8 cold savories *8–12 items each*	5 cold savories 3 hot savories *8–12 items each*	3 cold canapés *3 items each* 2 cold fork dishes 2 salads 1 bread 1 cold dessert	2 cold canapés 1 hot canapé *3 items each* 1 cold fork dish 1 hot fork dish 1 cold salad 1 hot vegetable dish 1 bread 1 cold dessert	2 cold fork dishes 1 salad 1 bread 1 cold dessert	1 cold fork dish 1 hot fork dish 1 salad 1 bread 1 cold dessert
50–60 PEOPLE	7 cold savories 1 cold sweet *8–12 items each*	4 cold savories 3 hot savories 1 cold sweet *8–12 items each*	3 cold canapés *3 items each* 2 cold fork dishes 1 hot fork dish 2 salads 1 bread 2 cold desserts	2 cold canapés 1 hot canapé *3 items each* 1 cold fork dish 1 hot fork dish 1 salad 1 hot vegetable dish 1 bread 2 cold desserts	3 cold fork dishes 2 salads 1 bread 2 cold desserts	1 cold fork dish 2 hot fork dishes 1 salad 1 hot vegetable dish 1 bread 1 cold dessert 1 hot dessert

is frenetic, you hurriedly shop for parties on the way home from work, and there is never enough time to cook, do not even think about choosing a menu needing lots of last-minute attention. Instead, deliberately plan one that can be prepared a day or two ahead and needs only a minimum of attention before serving.

There are some ground rules about good menu planning. Think about all of the following when using the chart.

● Have a varied mix of ingredients, including fish and meat; dairy products; pasta, rice, or grains; and some fruits and vegetables too.

● Try not to repeat ingredients in the same menu, such as serving chicken twice, say, in a canapé topping and again in a salad.

● Have a contrast of textures, soft and crisp, as well as smooth and coarse.

● Include a good spectrum of colors in the menu, from pale and interesting foods to bold and bright.

● You will not want to have the entire range of these flavors in one menu, but think carefully about a balance of sweet versus sour, savory or bitter, salty or sharp, as well as smoky and flowery.

Entertaining will always be enjoyable if you are smart and stay within your capabilities and preferences. But do not be afraid to break the rules. Or, make up your own rules and do what you feel most comfortable with. And do not hesitate to make use of the local delicatessen — offering guests your favorite take-out foods plus a few homemade dishes should be no reason for guilt.

Make the best of all that is in season too, for reasons of taste and economy. Budget must be a major factor when planning a menu, as ultimately it will affect what you can and cannot afford to

serve. Generally, the more choice you offer, the more it is going to cost you. So, if you are feeling particularly poor, why not just serve one great soup, a hunk of rustic bread, and a single, perfectly ripe cheese? That is not in the chart, but didn't I just say "break the rules"? Remember, the chart is simply a guideline to give you a helping hand.

Calculating quantities

Calculating quantities of food for a party is never an easy thing to do. A lot depends on the type of party, who is coming, the time of day, and many other factors.

Determining quantities for buffets when there is a large choice is probably the most difficult. Generally, the more people you are feeding, the less you will need to allow per head. You have to assume that everyone will have a little of everything, but not knowing which dish will be the popular one means you have to allow extra to compensate.

A useful tip if you are unsure is to take out the serving dishes you plan to use and think, for example, "That will serve ten people." Then, when you go shopping, you can visualize the amounts needed to fill that dish. Remember that it is always better to have too much than too little, and you can always eat it the following day. As for the range of dishes you should offer, I strongly believe that less is best. Fewer dishes make more impact on the table and on the plate. It will also strain your budget and resources less. The chart opposite will help you calculate quantities.

Advance preparation

Freezing prepared food for parties has lots of advantages. It means that if you know that time is going to be tight on the day of

When you know time will be scarce on the day of the party, choose a menu for which most of the dishes can be prepared in advance and frozen. Frequent hosts can regularly double the quantities of recipes and freeze in batches to save time.

the event, and you choose your recipes well, you can get ahead by freezing the bulk of the menu, or certainly some of the component parts. If you are a regular party giver, double up on your favorite recipes and freeze them to save time, energy, and expense, particularly with seasonal foods. The freezer is also a real asset for party leftovers, as long as they have not been previously frozen.

Most foods freeze well, but for best results, it is important to freeze them quickly. Make sure that hot dishes are completely cold before you wrap and freeze them. Use plastic freezer bags, foil bags, lidded foil containers, and sturdy plastic freezer containers with lids to store foods and to prevent freezer burn. Freeze liquids, such as soups, sauces, and drinks, in freezer bags placed in square containers. Then freeze them until solid, turn out, and return to the freezer. It is

Food quantities

FINGER FOODS

The following amounts are per person

Canapés

● Allow 4 to 6 bite-sized canapés for each hour that the party will last.

● If guests are going to be at the party for more than 3 hours, offer something more substantial, like bruschetta, to eat towards the end, since canapés are never a substitute for a full meal.

Finger buffet

● Allow 8 to 12 substantial finger food items, if it is a substitute for a meal.

FORK FOODS

The following amounts are per person

Poultry, meat, and fish *trimmed/boned weight*

● 6 oz when you only have 1 main dish.

● 8 oz when you have more than 2 or 3 main dishes. For example, if you were serving chicken and fish you would allow 4 oz of each, and if you were serving 3 dishes you would allow 3 oz of each.

● 2 oz poultry, meat, or fish; 2 oz rice, grains, lentils, pasta, or noodles; and 2 oz vegetables for a single main-course one-pot dish

Potatoes *unpeeled weight*

● 4 oz new potatoes (if leaving skins on), or 6 oz old potatoes, to accompany a single main course.

● 3 oz new potatoes (if leaving skins on), or 4 oz old potatoes, when 2 to 3 main courses and salads or vegetables are being served.

Vegetables *prepared weight*

● 4 oz for most vegetables, unless they have a lot of stalk or need a lot of peeling, such as root vegetables, when you would need to double the amount, to accompany a single main course.

● 2 oz when 2 to 3 main courses and salads or vegetables are being served.

Rice, grains, and lentils *uncooked weight*

● 1½ oz rice, grains, or lentils to accompany a single fish, meat, or poultry main course.

● 1½ oz rice for a first-course risotto.

● 2 oz rice for a main-course risotto.

● 1 oz rice, grains, or lentils when 2 to 3 main courses and salads or vegetables are being served.

● 2 oz rice, grains, or lentils; 2½ oz poultry, meat, or fish; and 2 oz vegetables for a single main-course one-pot dish.

Beans *uncooked weight*

● 2 oz to accompany a single fish, meat, or poultry main course.

● 1 oz when 2 or 3 main courses and salads or vegetables are being served.

Pasta and noodles *uncooked weight*

● 3 oz for a first course.

● 4 oz for a single main course.

● 2 oz to accompany a single main course.

● 1 oz when 2 to 3 main courses, salads, or vegetables are being served.

Leaf Salads

● 1 oz unprepared weight, or ½ oz prepared weight mixed salad leaves, to accompany a first course, main course, buffet, or cheese course.

Butter

● ½ oz to serve with bread or crackers and cheese.

Cheese

● 4 oz if serving on its own, or 2 oz when you are serving a dessert as well.

Desserts

● 5 oz prepared weight fruit.

● A generous slice of pastry, tart, or cake.

● 4 oz mousses or creamy desserts.

● 5 oz ice cream.

● When you are serving two desserts — such as a fruit dish and a mousse — allow slightly more than half the total quantities of each. For example, 4 oz fruit and 3 oz mousse.

important that meat, poultry, and fish are defrosted in the fridge to prevent the growth of any harmful bacteria, but most other foods can be defrosted at room temperature, out of sunlight. Refer to the individual recipes in this book for details of how long to freeze particular dishes and how best to reheat or complete them.

Serving

When you are inviting lots of people over, you should consider having buffet tables at both ends of the room to avoid everyone congregating in one place. Make sure, though, that wherever you site these tables, there is an easy route to bring food through from the kitchen. If you have the space, allow a separate table for the dessert, plates, and cutlery and put it all out in advance of the meal. People eat at different speeds, and you may find that some of them are ready to move on to the dessert while others are still eating their main course. Never put a buffet table and a bar table next to each other, as you will find that this arrangement will cause a major bottleneck.

If time or space is tight, there are occasions when I do not set up a buffet table at all. Instead, I individually plate all the food in the kitchen, and if I am serving two or three main courses, I send out a selection of them on very large trays. The wait staff makes sure that each tray has a good range of dishes on it so that there is something for everyone, with a meat, a fish, and a vegetarian option. Forks get put on to the sides of plates, and napkins all get piled in the center of the tray.

When you are using buffet tables, set out plates, cutlery, and the same array of food at the start, middle, and end of the table to avoid bottlenecks and delays.

To prevent your guests from needlessly lining up at the buffet table, do not make a big announcement that the food is ready. Instead, invite small groups of people, say ten at a time, to come up to the table and get their food. I always like to have some help serving buffet dishes, as it means you can control the amount of food being served (particularly useful for occasions when you have accidentally under-catered), and these helpers can keep relays of dishes coming from the kitchen so that the food is hot for everyone.

If you are planning to have a seated fork buffet, often a cold first course can be plated in advance and put on the table

Cocktail parties are a marvelous way to show off your individual style if you choose decorations and serving dishes to suit. This is an amusing yet practical way to offer round small cones of fish and chips, invariably a popular choice of canapé.

just before everyone sits down to the meal. Guests can then come up to the buffet table and help themselves to the main course and, later on, to the dessert. Alternatively, the dessert can be plated and then served by helpers, if you do not want your friends bobbing up and down too much during the meal.

At a stand-up buffet, I sometimes go around with platters of food in case anyone is ravenous and wants a second helping, which saves them having to return to the table to get it themselves.

Finger food only

English Cocktail Party Menu

- Radishes with Watercress Butter *p42*
- Cheddar Scones with Mustard
  Butter & Ham *p48*
- Sausage & Mash Croustades *p50*
- Quail Egg & Smoked Salmon Tartlets *p57*
- Fish & Chips *p74*
- Whisky Sours *p154*

Saffron mussels in garlic bread

Mediterranean Cocktail Party Menu

- Celery with Olive & Parsley Salad *p42*
- Cheddar Crackers, Goat Cheese, Tomatoes
  & Basil *p56*
- Camembert Ice Cream on Parmesan
  Toasts *p53*
- Saffron Mussels in Garlic Bread *p53*
- Deep-Fried Sage Leaves with Anchovies *p74*
- Italian Vegetable Skewers *p76*
- Negronis *p157*

Fish & chips

Fork food only

Family Lunch Menu

- Zucchini & Seafood Salad *p100*
- Chicken Scaloppine with Mozzarella
  & Sage *p97*
- Roasted Vegetables *p130*
  (omit the roasted tomatoes)
- Baked Peaches with Figs, Ginger &
  Spices *p132*

Baked peaches with figs, ginger & spices

suggested menus

Yogurt ices

Here are a few themed menus to get you thinking about what food and drinks you might like to serve at your party. You can follow them closely, or use them as a base and add your own ideas, bearing in mind the rules of good menu planning mentioned on page 23. More delicious menus can be found on the feature pages in the recipe chapters of this book.

Children's Birthday Party Menu

- Garlic Potato Chips *p39*
- Hamburgers *p48*
- Sausages & Parsley Mash *p36*
- Fish & Chips *p74*
- Vermicelli Shrimp on Chinese Seaweed *p74*
- Yogurt Ices *p83*
- Happy Birthday Cupcakes *p85*
- Lime, Orange & Lemon Pressés *p148*

Zucchini & seafood salad

Do-Ahead Menu

- Saffron Lamb Tagine with Couscous *p95*
- Arugula, French Beans, Red Onion & Croûton Salad *p128*
- Apricot Tart *p135*

One-Hour Menu

- Thai Mussels *p102*
- Green Salad *p126*
- Saffron Cream with Sesame–Poppy Seed Wafers *p137*

Thai mussels

Wedding Menu

- Roast Beef Salad *p95*
- Zucchini & Seafood Salad *p100*
- Chicken Tonnato Salad *p96*
- Tabbouleh Primavera *p112*
- Potato, Watercress & Walnut Salad *p129*
- Tomato Salad *p126*
- Rolled Pavlova with Mango & Passion Fruit *p133*
- Red Berry Kissel with Biscotti & Vanilla Cream *p132*
- Heart Cake with Rose Petals *p141*
- Long Island Iced Tea *p154*
- Limey *p149*

Mozzarella salad with olives, anchovies & parsley

Vegetarian Special Occasion Menu

- Green Mango & Papaya Salad *p127*
- Asian Ravioli with Soy-Butter Sauce *p118*
- Stir-fried Bok Choy, Asparagus & Sugar Snaps *p130*
- Lime & Pistachio Kulfi with Pistachio Wafers *p139*
- Simply Red *p157*

Finger and fork food

All-American Menu

- Belgian Endive with Roquefort, Pecans & Cranberries *p42*
- Cornmeal Muffins with Maryland Crab Cakes *p51*
- Jambalaya *p116*
- Green Salad *p126*
- Tomato Salad *p126*
- Apple & Blackberry Filo Pastries *p134*
- Mint Juleps *p154*

Belgian Endive with Roquefort, pecans & cranberries

Glamorous Menu

- Caviar Eclairs *p55*
- Quail Egg & Smoked Salmon Tartlets *p57*
- Brioches Filled with Wild Mushrooms *p53*
- Seared Salmon, Asparagus & Potato Salad *p100*
- Cucumber, Sugar Snap & Radish Salad *p126*
- Scarlet & Green Beans *p131*
- Raspberry & Lemon Syllabub Trifle *p136*
- Champagne & Sorbet Fizz *p154*

Light & Healthy Menu

- Vietnamese Chicken Salad *p96*
  (omit the Napa cabbage)
- Mozzarella with Olives, Anchovies & Parsley *p129*
- Asian Coleslaw *p127*
- Elderflower Jellies *p78*
- Kiwi Cooler *p152*

At parties, drinks deserve as much attention as food. For some, it might just be a well-chosen wine, a few icy cold beers, or a fabulous fruity cocktail. These days, apart from making sure that everyone is happily taken care of, there are no rigid rules about what you should and should not serve. However, there will be some occasions when you want to offer a wider range of drinks, so refer to the charts on these pages. They will help you plan the quantities and chilling and bar equipment needed.

Whatever drinks you decide to serve at the party, keep them simple. People do not want to be offered a vast array of refreshments, and apart from that, you will find it expensive and demanding to provide a fully stocked bar.

The starting point should be the type of party you are having and the drinking habits of your guests. There could be young, old, teetotalers, those who insist on their favorite tipple, and others who are content to drink anything offered.

To set up a bar, you ideally need a 6-foot-long table or counter for each 50 to 75 guests. Protect any precious surfaces by covering them with plastic wrap before putting down the tablecloth. Then put plastic sheeting beneath the table to protect the floor.

If you do not have a large enough fridge to chill all your drinks, you will

drinks and the bar

	20 GUESTS		40 GUESTS		60 GUESTS		
	2 hours	3 hours	2 hours	3 hours	2 hours	3 hours	
CHAMPAGNE PARTY							
Champagne/ Sparkling wine	9 x 750ml bottles	14 x 750ml bottles	17 x 750ml bottles	27 x 750ml bottles	25 x 750ml bottles	40 x 750ml bottles	
WINE PARTY							
White wine	7 x 750ml bottles	11 x 750ml bottles	16 x 750ml bottles	22 x 750ml bottles	20 x 750ml bottles	32 x 750ml bottles	Finger-food party
Red wine	3 x 750ml bottles	5 x 750ml bottles	6 x 750ml bottles	10 x 750ml bottles	10 x 750ml bottles	16 x 750ml bottles	
CHAMPAGNE OR WINE PARTY							
Soft drinks	3.5 liters	6 liters	7 liters	11 liters	14 liters	18 liters	
Mineral water	5 liters	8 liters	10 liters	15 liters	15 liters	22 liters	

	20 GUESTS	40 GUESTS	60 GUESTS	
WINE PARTY				
White wine	8 x 750ml bottles	16 x 750ml bottles	24 x 750ml bottles	
Red wine	4 x 750ml bottles	8 x 750ml bottles	12 x 750ml bottles	Fork-food party
Soft drinks	3.5 liters	7 liters	14 liters	
Mineral water	7 liters	14 liters	20 liters	

need to allow 1 lb ice per person, which is enough for chilling bottles and for adding to drinks. On very hot days, or if the party is going to go on for many hours, allow more. Chill everything in a clean trash can or similar deep waterproof container that will take 30 lb of ice and about 36 bottles. Put this on the plastic sheeting, along with a trash can for empties. Layer up the bottles with ice and add some cold water, particularly if you are in a hurry, to speed the chilling process, which will take about 1 hour.

To save time when serving later, open still wines, push the cork back into the bottle, and chill. If you are having a large party, try to chill the drinks in separate containers, as you will find it faster to dispense them. Store ice for putting into drinks in a separate ice bucket to avoid contamination. Make crushed ice by putting ice cubes in a clean dish towel and hitting them with a rolling pin.

You will need twice as many glasses as people as they get abandoned easily. Choose the glass to match the drink: flutes for champagne; a generous wine glass for wines, juice, and water; straight-sided highballs for tall drinks served with ice; tumblers for spirits and juices; V-shaped glasses for cocktails; balloon glasses for brandy. In the end though, unless renting glasses, we all make do with what we have. You can get away with just champagne and wineglasses.

Ideally, for a bar for 50 guests, you will also need 5 cocktail trays, an ice bucket, a wine cooler, 3 pitchers, a bowl for garnishes, and 6 waiters' napkins. Make sure you have the equipment listed in the checklist on page 21, too. Scale the quantities of equipment up or down according to the number of guests.

Calculating quantities

Champagne or sparkling wine:
There are 6 champagne flutes to a 750ml bottle. For a 2-hour cocktail party, if the only other drinks you are serving are mineral water and soft drinks, allow 2½ glasses each. As an aperitif before dinner, allow 1½ glasses per person. At weddings, when you want to toast the bride and groom, a single glass each is sufficient. A single glass is also enough to serve with dessert. When you are diluting champagne or sparkling wine with a fruit purée, allow about 8 glasses per bottle.

Wines:
There are about 5 medium wineglasses to a 750ml bottle. For a 2-hour cocktail party, if you are not serving anything else, apart from mineral water and soft drinks, allow 1 bottle for 2 people. At cocktail parties, white wine is generally more popular than red, so have two-thirds white to one-third red. For fork lunches or suppers, allow 2 glasses of white wine and 1½ glasses of red each. If you are providing only red or white, 3 glasses will generally be enough.

Spirits and Mixers:
A 750ml bottle will make about 17 single measures, served in old-fashioned tumblers. If you are only serving spirits or cocktails, mineral water and juice at a 2-hour cocktail party, you probably need to allow 3 per person. The range of spirits to offer is purely personal, but these days it is more usual to find a basic bar of gin, whisky, and vodka, as well as wines and beers, rather than a fully stocked bar. However, if you do want a fuller bar you could add tequila, brandy, Campari, rum, bourbon, vermouth, and sherry.

The obligatory mixers are orange juice, soda, tonic, ginger ale, tomato juice, and cola. Do not forget to provide lemons for mixing and slicing, any other garnishes, and bottles of Tabasco and Worcestershire sauce for pepping up tomato juice.

Liqueurs:
A 750ml bottle of liqueur, such as Armagnac, other brandy, Cointreau, or similar, will give about 15 liqueur or brandy glasses for an after-dinner drink. You should only need 1 per person.

Mineral water:
Each 1-liter bottle yields about 5 glasses. For a 2-hour cocktail party, provide 1 bottle for every 4 guests. Remember that some will prefer still water to sparkling, so you will need to allow an appropriate amount. For a fork lunch or supper, a bottle for every 3 guests will be enough.

Soft drinks:
At a 2-hour cocktail party, when you are serving champagne or wine along with mineral water, you need to have some soft drinks. A glass, or about 6 oz of juice each, will do. But for parties at which you are only going to serve soft drinks and no alcohol whatsoever, allow a total of about 3 glasses each.

finger

FOOD

Whether it is a **few snacks** for a casual party with friends or a stunning **style statement** accompanied with fine wines, **spirits,** and your best outfit or suit, here you'll find **all you need** to know about producing **great nibbles**. Inspiration comes from the **food jet set**, with fresh flavors flown in from the **Far East**, the Americas, Europe, and the Mediterranean. We start at the very beginning, with **really easy** dishes requiring **no cooking** and antipasto ideas more about **good shopping** than **chef-class** cookery techniques. But for those times when you want to show off, there is also a selection of **eye-opening**, mouth-dropping, lip-smacking **canapés with wit**. Not sure how to put it all together? The **feature** pages have stylish ideas for **romantic** weddings, **informal** housewarmings, and **classy** cocktail dos. Easy on the cook, delicious on the guests, this food is **finger-licking** fantastic.

Olives, feta & chilies

A colorful array of Mediterranean ingredients that takes a matter of minutes to assemble. SERVES 10

1½ cups mixed olives, such as black niçoise, purple kalamata & green stuffed with almonds
4 oz feta cheese, crumbled
½ cup pickled hot chilies, drained
A few basil leaves

Toss all the ingredients together in a bowl and serve.

Advance preparation: Assemble up to 5 hours ahead, adding the basil just before serving.
Freezing: Not suitable.

Spoon canapés

The perfect way to serve prime ingredients and show off any pretty or unusual spoons that you have. MAKES 30

for the crab & lemon
4 oz fresh lump crabmeat
2 tsp fresh lemon juice
Salt to taste
1 scallion, finely sliced
for the gingered oysters
10 fresh oysters
2 tblsp rice wine or white wine vinegar
2-inch piece fresh ginger, cut into fine strips
for the caviar & crème fraîche
⅓ cup crème fraîche
2 ounces sevruga caviar
You will also need 30 spoons

Season the crabmeat with the lemon juice and salt. Arrange it on 10 of the spoons and garnish with the scallion.
Divide the oysters among 10 spoons and sprinkle with the vinegar and ginger.
Place the crème fraîche on the remaining spoons and top with the caviar.
Arrange them all on a platter and serve.

Advance preparation: Cut the scallion and ginger up to 8 hours before, cover,

left Olives, feta & chilies

and chill. Arrange the ingredients on the spoons up to 30 minutes before, cover, and keep chilled.
Freezing: Not suitable.

Bagel crisps & pink peppercorn gravlax

Pink peppercorns give the salmon a splash of color and a touch of heat. MAKES 10

4 oz sliced gravlax (smoked salmon)
10 bagel crisps
2 tsp dried pink peppercorns, crushed
2 limes, halved lengthwise

Cut the salmon into 10 pieces and arrange them in rosettes on the bagels.
Scatter over the peppercorns and serve with the limes for guests to squeeze.

Advance preparation: Top the bagels and cut the limes up to 1 hour ahead. Cover and chill.
Freezing: Not suitable.

Vodka cherry tomatoes with herbed garlic salt

Add the leftover vodka marinade to a jug of bloody Marys or some Oyster Shooters (page 156). The garlic salt will keep for ages in a screw-topped jar and is terrific sprinkled on meat, fish, poultry, and vegetables before grilling or roasting. SERVES 10

for the vodka tomatoes
1½ cups red & yellow cherry tomatoes
⅔ cup vodka
1 tblsp Worcestershire sauce
12 drops Tabasco sauce
1 clove garlic, crushed
for the herbed garlic salt
⅓ cup fine sea salt
Grated zest of ½ lemon
1 tsp black peppercorns, crushed
1 heaping tsp chopped fresh rosemary
1 small clove garlic, crushed

Cut a small cross in the base of each tomato and place in a bowl.
Stir the vodka, the Worcestershire and Tabasco sauces, and the garlic into the

bowl of tomatoes. Cover and marinate in the fridge for 24 hours.
Mix all the ingredients together for the herbed garlic salt and let infuse for at least 2 hours.
Drain the tomatoes, reserving the liquid for another recipe. Serve with the flavored salt for dipping.

Advance preparation: The tomatoes can be marinated 2 days in advance; the herbed salt can be made weeks ahead.
Freezing: Not suitable.

Shrimp chips & Chinese salsa

This is a ten-minute recipe for when you are in a real hurry. SERVES 10

20 shrimp or root vegetable chips
for the Chinese salsa
1 tsp finely grated fresh ginger
1 tblsp light soy sauce
1 tblsp toasted sesame seeds
¼ green bell pepper, seeded and coarsely chopped
¼ yellow bell pepper, seeded and coarsely chopped
1 red bird's-eye chili, seeded & finely chopped
1 tblsp toasted sesame oil

Mix all the salsa ingredients together to make a wet paste and serve in a bowl alongside the chips for dipping.

Spoon canapés

Advance preparation: Make the salsa up to 4 hours before, cover, and keep cool.
Freezing: Not suitable.

Rice crackers with crispy vegetables

I also like to top Japanese rice crackers with shrimp and a dollop of plain yogurt flavored with some ground cumin and coriander. MAKES 10

10 Japanese rice crackers
for the vegetables
¼ small red bell pepper, seeded and finely sliced
¼ small yellow bell pepper, seeded and finely sliced
1 small carrot, finely sliced
3 snow peas, finely sliced
A few shiso leaves to garnish
for the dressing
1 tsp rice wine vinegar
A pinch of salt
A pinch of sugar
3 drops Tabasco sauce

Mix the sliced vegetables in a bowl with the vinegar, salt, sugar, and Tabasco.
Spoon onto the rice crackers and garnish with the shiso leaves. Serve them within 30 minutes of topping.

Advance preparation: Cut the vegetables 1 day before and store separately in the fridge in plastic wrap.
Freezing: Not suitable.

Mediterranean antipasto

What could be simpler than an assortment of everyday Mediterranean ingredients presented on a platter? Include a selection of salami, one fine textured, one coarse, and another hot and spicy. A pot of rillettes, or thick slice of pâté, would not go amiss here, served with some good bread. SERVES 10

20 slices mixed salami, such as
   milanese, calabrese & soppressata
10 bocconcini (tiny mozzarella)
8 oz drained bottled artichokes in oil,
   drained
1 cup radishes
⅓ cup caperberries or capers, drained
1 cup olives

Arrange all the ingredients on a platter and serve.

Advance preparation: Arrange up to 4 hours ahead, cover, and chill.
Freezing: Not suitable.

Asian antipasto

Fill the tomatoes with basil pesto if you prefer. Crispy Duck Pancakes (page 41), made without chives, are a good addition to this platter, as are quail eggs (page 36), dipped into the Szechwan salt. SERVES 10

5 oz asparagus
10 large cooked shrimp, shelled and
   deveined
for the cilantro roasted tomatoes
5 Roma (plum) tomatoes, halved
   lengthwise
2 tblsp olive oil
A large pinch of sugar
Cilantro Pesto (page 43), or ⅓ cup
   ready-made pesto
Salt & freshly ground pepper to taste
for the gingered mushrooms
3 tblsp toasted sesame oil
5 oz fresh shiitake mushrooms
1 tsp finely grated fresh ginger
for the Szechwan salt
1½ tblsp fine sea salt

1 tsp Szechwan peppercorns, seeded
for the wontons
Vegetable oil for deep-frying
10 wonton wrappers
A pinch of salt
½ tsp five-spice powder
*A large and small square of banana leaf,
to serve (optional)*

Preheat the oven to 375°F. Put the tomatoes skin-side down in a roasting pan, drizzle with olive oil, and sprinkle with the sugar, salt, and pepper. **Roast** the tomatoes for 30 minutes or until soft and slightly charred. Remove from the pan while warm, lift onto paper towels, cool, and top with the pesto.

Boil the asparagus for 2–3 minutes in a pan of salted water or until al dente. Drain under cold water and dry on paper towels.

Heat the sesame oil in a pan. Sauté the mushrooms and ginger for 3–4 minutes. Drain, cool, and season with salt.

Stir the sea salt and Szechwan pepper-

Mediterranean antipasto

corns over a medium heat for 1 minute or until smoking. Cool, grind briefly, and place on a small square of banana leaf, or in a bowl, for dipping the shrimp.

Heat the vegetable oil in a large pan to 350°F. Fry the wonton wrappers for 30 seconds or until golden, drain, and cool. Dust with the salt and five-spice.

Arrange everything on a plate lined with a large square of banana leaf and serve.

Advance preparation: Two days before, make the Szechwan salt and store in an airtight jar; roast the tomatoes, cool, and chill. Cook the asparagus and mushrooms 1 day before, cover, and chill. Fry the wonton wrappers 12 hours before and store in an airtight container. Fill the tomatoes and assemble the platter 1 hour before. *Freezing: Not suitable.*

Middle Eastern antipasto

Dukkah is an Egyptian mixture of crushed nuts and spices. Dip the flat bread into the oil and then into the dukkah. SERVES 10

Moroccan Meatballs (page 40)
Sesame Cheese Straws (page 54)
Olives, Feta & Chilies (page 32)
⅓ cup olive oil
2 large sheets Lebanese flat bread, torn
for the dukkah
⅓ cup almonds or hazelnuts
¾ cup white sesame seeds
¼ cup coriander seeds
¼ cup cumin seeds
Salt & freshly ground pepper to taste

Toast the nuts and spices over high heat for 1 minute, stirring constantly.
Crush the nuts and spices, then season.
Arrange the dukkah in a bowl on a platter with a bowl of oil for dipping the flat bread, plus the assembled dishes of meatballs, sesame straws, and olives.

Advance preparation: Toast the nuts and spices 4 hours ahead and cover. Assemble the platter 1 hour before serving. *Freezing: Not suitable.*

right Asian antipasto

Quail eggs with roasted sesame salt

You have to like your friends a lot to shell quail eggs for them! SERVES 10

36 quail eggs
1 heaping tblsp white sesame seeds
A pinch of cayenne pepper
A pinch of cumin
1 heaping tblsp fine sea salt
A pinch of ground pepper

Put the eggs into a pan of boiling water. Boil for 2 minutes 45 seconds for soft-boiled, 3 minutes for hard-boiled. Drain under running cold water until cold.

Reserve a few eggs in their shells to garnish. Shell the rest, rinse, dry on paper towels, and put into a serving dish.

Toast the remaining ingredients over low heat for 2–3 minutes. Cool, put into a small dish, and serve with the quail eggs.

Advance preparation: Make the salt dip 1 week ahead and store in an airtight jar. Cook and shell the eggs 1 day before, cover, and chill.
Freezing: Not suitable.

Sausages & parsley mash

Make this old-fashioned favorite for lunch or supper as well as cocktail parties. SERVES 10

1 lb pork cocktail sausages
2 tblsp vegetable oil
for the parsley mash
1 lb boiling potatoes, quartered
1½ cups flat-leaf parsley sprigs
3 tblsp olive oil
2 tblsp heavy cream

Cook the potatoes in a pan of salted water for 15–20 minutes or until tender. Drain and mash until smooth.

Heat the olive oil and cream in a pan to just below boiling point, then pour into a blender or processor with the parsley. Blend until the parsley is coarsely chopped.

Stir the parsley mixture into the potato purée, season well, and cover with foil.

Preheat the oven to 375°F. Roast the sausages in the vegetable oil for 20–25 minutes or until brown. Reheat the mash in the oven for 15 minutes.

Drain the sausages on paper towels and serve with the parsley mash as a dip.

Advance preparation: Make the parsley mash 2 days before, cover, and chill.
Freezing: Freeze the mash 4 weeks before.

Bean brandade crudités

This garlicky bean brandade can also be used as a bruschetta topping. SERVES 10

for the bean brandade
1½ cups canned cannellini beans, drained
1 large clove garlic, crushed
2 tblsp fresh lemon juice

Quail eggs with roasted sesame salt

½ cup olive oil
2 tblsp heavy cream
2 tblsp coarsely chopped fresh parsley
Salt & freshly ground pepper to taste
for the crudités
⅓ cup dry white wine
1 small clove garlic, crushed
8 oz small fresh mussels
1 lb small fresh clams
2 heads red or yellow chicory
1 head radicchio
2 bunches dandelion greens
10 baby fennel bulbs
1 lb small carrots
8 oz broccoli rabe or broccoli

Reserve a third of the beans. Purée the rest in a blender or processor with the garlic, lemon juice, oil, cream, parsley and seasoning.

Add the reserved beans and pulse until coarsely chopped and combined with the rest of the mixture. Transfer to a bowl.
Heat the wine and garlic in a large pan over a high heat, add the mussels and clams, cover, and steam for 4–5 minutes or until all the shells have opened. Discard any that are unopened. Remove with a slotted spoon and cool.
Separate the salad leaves and arrange them with the vegetables and shellfish on a platter with the brandade.

Advance preparation: Make the bean brandade up to 3 days ahead, cover, and chill. Steam the shellfish up to 6 hours before, cover, and chill. Assemble up to 4 hours ahead, cover, and chill.
Freezing: Not suitable.

Grissini & rouille dip

Rouille also makes a vibrant dressing for chicken salads or pasta. SERVES 10

for the grissini
1 cup all-purpose flour, sifted + extra for rolling
1 pkg rapid-rise dry yeast
A pinch of salt
3 tblsp warm water
1 tblsp olive oil + extra for greasing
1 tblsp coarsely chopped fresh parsley
2 tblsp coarsely chopped black olives
2 tsp finely chopped hot red chilies
1 tsp fine sea salt
for the rouille
2 oz white bread, crusts removed
4½ tblsp olive oil
15 oz canned pimientos, drained, rinsed, and coarsely chopped
2 cloves garlic, crushed
Salt & freshly ground pepper to taste

Mix the flour, yeast, and salt together. Stir in the water and oil to make a soft dough, adding more water if needed.
Knead for 5 minutes or until smooth. Place in a bowl, cover, and leave in a warm place for 1 hour or until doubled in size.
Divide the dough into 4 and add the parsley to one quarter, olives to another, chili to the third, and leave the last plain.
Knead to incorporate the flavorings and divide each of the doughs into 5 pieces.
Preheat the oven to 375°F. Roll each batch of dough out on a lightly floured surface and cut them thinly into 8- to 10-inch-long grissini. Sprinkle the salt over the final unflavored batch.
Place on lightly oiled baking sheets and bake for 8–10 minutes or until crisp and golden. Transfer to a wire rack to cool.
Soak the bread for the rouille in the oil for 10 minutes. Purée the pimientos and garlic in a processor. Gradually add the soaked bread and blend until smooth. Season and serve in a bowl with the grissini for dipping.

Advance preparation: Make the rouille up to 2 days before, cover, and chill.
Freezing: Make and freeze the grissini up to 4 weeks before.

Masala potato wedges

The heat of these spicy potatoes is balanced by a fruity tamarind ketchup. SERVES 10

for the masala potato wedges
¼ cup water
¼ cup tomato paste
¼ cup fresh lemon juice
½ tsp hot chili powder
1 tblsp ground coriander
2 tsp ground cumin
2 tsp salt
¼ cup vegetable oil
5 unpeeled potatoes, cut lengthwise into 6 pieces
for the Indian ketchup
1 tsp brown mustard seeds
1 tblsp toasted sesame oil
2 cloves garlic, crushed
½ tsp ground cardamom
½ tsp finely grated fresh ginger
A pinch of ground cinnamon
A pinch of ground cloves
½ tsp cayenne pepper
¼ cup packed dark brown sugar
½ tsp salt
2 tblsp concentrated tamarind paste
1 lb canned chopped tomatoes

Preheat the oven to 350°F. Whisk the water, tomato paste, lemon juice, spices, and salt into a paste.
Pour the oil into a roasting pan, add the potatoes, then spoon over the paste and stir to coat well. Bake for 25 minutes or until cooked through and dark golden, shaking the potatoes from time to time.
Fry the mustard seeds for the ketchup in the sesame oil over medium heat for about 30 seconds. Lower the heat and stir in the garlic, all the spices, sugar, and salt. Cook for 1 minute, stirring.
Add the tamarind and tomatoes. Simmer for 10–15 minutes until thick.
Cool the ketchup, then spoon it into a serving bowl. Serve the hot potato wedges with the ketchup to dip.

Advance preparation: Make the ketchup up to 5 days before, cover, and chill.
Freezing: Freeze the ketchup up to 4 weeks before. Simmer for 5 minutes if it needs thickening after being defrosted.

Poppadums & chutneys

I like to supplement ordinary shop-bought poppadums with some different varieties from my favorite Indian restaurant, such as the flowerlike achappams and pappadavadai, which are dipped in a spiced rice flour batter. If you do want to make your own dip, the Indian ketchup (page 35) is an authentic partner. SERVES 10

Two 16-oz jars Indian chutney or
  pickles, such as mango, lime, or
  eggplant
Vegetable oil for deep-frying
20 spiced poppadums

Spoon the chutney or pickles into bowls.
Heat the oil in a deep-fat fryer or large pan to 350°F. Fry the poppadums one at a time in the oil for 30–40 seconds or until crisp and golden. Drain on paper towels. Alternatively, toast them under a preheated broiler on both sides for a total of about 20-30 seconds or until puffy.
Serve hot or cold with the chutney.

Advance preparation: Cook the poppadums 1 day ahead and store in an airtight container. Reheat in a warm oven.
Freezing: Not suitable.

Garlic potato chips

Potato chips are addictive enough, but tossing them in hot garlic butter makes them even more so. Since they will disappear in a flash, make more than you could possibly imagine your friends eating. SERVES 10

1¼ lb potato chips
for the garlic butter
⅔ cup (1⅓ sticks) butter
1 large clove garlic, crushed
2 heaping tblsp chopped fresh parsley
Salt & freshly ground pepper to taste

Put the chips on a shallow ovenproof dish or baking sheet.
Melt the butter, add the garlic, and cook over low heat for 30 seconds, then add

lots of salt and some pepper. Cool a little, stir in the parsley, pour over the chips, and toss so that they are well coated.
Heat through for 3–5 minutes in a preheated 350°F oven and serve.

Advance preparation: The chips can be tossed in the garlic butter up to 1 day ahead, stored in an airtight container, and kept in a cool place. Heat as above.
Freezing: Make the garlic-parsley butter and freeze up to 4 weeks before.

Lacquered sesame nuts

This recipe is adapted from the one in Yan Kit-So's excellent book **Classic Food of China.** *I've added unlacquered macadamias and pistachios for variety.* SERVES 10

2 cups (9 oz) cashew nuts
3 tblsp sugar
6 tblsp light corn syrup
Vegetable oil for deep-frying
2 tsp roasted white sesame seeds
¾ cup (3 oz) macadamia nuts
¾ cup (3 oz) shelled pistachio nuts
You will also need a cooking thermometer

Put the cashews in a saucepan, cover with water, and boil for 5 minutes, skimming as necessary. Drain.
Return the cashews to the pan, pour over 6 cups boiling water, add the sugar, and boil 5 minutes, stirring occasionally. Drain again.
Heat the same pan for 1 minute or until hot, then remove it from the heat and add the still-hot cashew nuts and the golden syrup. Mix well to glaze every nut.
Put the pan back onto a medium heat and stir for 20–30 seconds before pouring the cashew nuts into a colander to drain off all the excess syrup.
Half-fill a medium pan or wok with oil and heat to 350°F. Carefully spoon the cashews into the hot oil, which will foam. Stir gently with a slotted spoon from time to time, frying for 7–8 minutes or until golden brown.
Remove the cashews with the slotted spoon, drain in a colander, and sprinkle over the sesame seeds. Shake to separate

the nuts before they cool and harden.
Toss the cold lacquered cashews with the macadamias and pistachios and serve.

Advance preparation: Make the lacquered cashews up to 2 weeks ahead and store in a cool place in an airtight container lined with parchment paper.
Freezing: Not suitable.

Vietnamese rice crackers with peanut sauce

In Vietnam, banh trang are normally moistened and used for spring rolls. Here they are deep-fried and served with a spicy peanut sauce also used in the bruschetta section as a sauce for chicken. SERVES 10

Vegetable oil for deep-frying
20 rice paper wrappers (banh trang)
for the peanut sauce
1 tblsp light soy sauce
1 tblsp toasted sesame oil
1 tblsp fresh lemon juice
1 tblsp honey
1 tblsp finely grated fresh ginger
3 heaping tblsp crunchy peanut butter
1 small red bird's-eye chili, seeded &
  finely diced
1 small clove garlic, crushed
¼ cup boiling water
1 tblsp peanuts, coarsely chopped

Put all the sauce ingredients, except for half the chili and the peanuts, into a blender or processor and pulse 7–8 times to blend.
Spoon into a bowl and scatter over the remaining chili and the peanuts.
Heat the oil in a deep-fat fryer or large pan to 350°F. Fry the rice paper wrappers one at a time in the hot oil for 30–40 seconds until or crisp and golden.
Drain on paper towels. Serve hot or cold with the peanut dipping sauce.

Advance preparation: Make the sauce 2 weeks ahead, cover, and chill. Cook the crackers 1 day in advance and store in an airtight container. Crisp in a warm oven.
Freezing: Make and freeze the sauce up to 4 weeks before.

Armenian bread, hummus & vegetables

This is a very fast wrap to make. Tzatziki is good used in place of hummus. SERVES 10

2 large sheets Armenian flat bread
3 rounded tblsp hummus
½ small red bell pepper, seeded and cut into strips
½ small yellow bell pepper, seeded and cut into strips
¼ cup pea or leek shoots

Preheat the oven to 350°F. Sprinkle the bread lightly with water and warm it in the oven for 1–2 minutes, but do not let it crisp. Let cool and cut into 5 x 4-inch strips.
Spread each strip of flat bread with hummus, leaving a border around the edges, and then divide the peppers and shoots between them.
Fold in the bottom end and roll up, letting the vegetables poke out at the top. Serve.

Advance preparation: Cut the peppers 4 hours ahead, cover, and chill. Wrap the bread 2 hours before, cover, and chill.
Freezing: Not suitable.

Lettuce-wrapped Moroccan meatballs

The aromatic Moroccan spice mixture, ras el hanout, used in these little meatballs is typically made with allspice, cinnamon, cloves, coriander and cumin seeds, ginger, and peppercorns. Pork can be used instead of lamb, although it's not a meat normally eaten in Morocco. SERVES 10

1 heaping tsp cornstarch
2 tblsp vegetable oil
10 baby romaine lettuce leaves
5 mint leaves
5 cilantro leaves
½ cup chili sauce
for the Moroccan meatballs
4 oz ground lamb or pork
1 scallion, chopped
2 tsp ras el hanout
2 tblsp chopped fresh cilantro
2 tblsp white sesame seeds
Salt & freshly ground pepper to taste

Lettuce-wrapped Moroccan meatballs

Mix all the ingredients together for the meatballs and roll into 20 balls.
Sprinkle the cornstarch on a tray and roll the balls in it to lightly coat.
Heat the oil in a frying pan and fry the meatballs in batches over medium heat for 3–4 minutes or until well browned.
Remove with a slotted spoon to drain on paper towels. Let them cool a little.
Put a warm meatball on each lettuce leaf and place a mint or cilantro leaf on top. Serve with the chili sauce to dip.

Advance preparation: Fry the meatballs 8 hours before, cool, cover, and chill. Reheat them at 375°F for 10 minutes or until hot. Prepare the lettuce, cilantro, and mint; cover, and chill up to 8 hours before.
Freezing: The meatballs can be frozen cooked or uncooked 4 weeks ahead.

Shiitake mushroom & ginger chopsticks

The mushroom filling in this recipe also makes a good ravioli stuffing. SERVES 10

1 tblsp cornstarch
20 wonton wrappers
Vegetable oil for deep-frying
Chinese plum sauce to dip
for the shiitake mushroom & ginger filling
6 tblsp toasted sesame oil
6 tblsp finely chopped shallots
8 oz fresh shiitake mushrooms, stemmed and coarsely chopped

1 clove garlic, crushed
2 tsp finely grated fresh ginger
1 tsp five-spice powder
Salt & freshly ground pepper to taste

Heat the sesame oil in a pan over medium heat, add the shallots, and fry for 2–3 minutes. Stir in the mushrooms, garlic, and ginger and cook for 6 minutes until softened. Season with five-spice powder, salt, and pepper. Set aside to cool.
Dust a work surface lightly with cornstarch and separate the wonton wrappers.
Brush a ½-inch strip of water along one side of a wonton wrapper. Lay another on top of this dampened edge, giving one long wrapper. Press together to seal, then repeat with the remaining wrappers.
Spoon some of the mushroom mixture down one of the long sides of each extended wonton wrapper, leaving a ½-inch gap at both ends.
Brush the opposite side and the ends lightly with water and then roll each wrapper away from you to make a long chopsticklike roll. Pinch the ends to seal.
Heat the vegetable oil to 350°F in a large pan or deep fryer. Fry the rolls in batches for 2–3 minutes or until crisp and golden. Drain on paper towels and cool. Serve with the plum sauce to dip.

Advance preparation: Fry the rolls up to 6 hours in advance and store chilled on a tray lined with paper towels and covered

with paper. Reheat at 400°F for 5–7 minutes. Alternatively, place on a tray dusted with cornstarch, cover, and chill for 4 hours before frying to order.
Freezing: Freeze the mushroom mixture up to 4 weeks ahead.

Crispy duck pancakes

You can either serve this dish so that guests assemble their own, or wrapped and ready-to-go as in this recipe. MAKES 10

1 tsp salt
Three 8-oz duck breasts
1 tsp five-spice powder
⅓ cup hoisin sauce
10 Chinese pancakes (mu shu wrappers)
5 scallions, sliced diagonally
½ cucumber, seeded & cut into thin strips
¼ cup bean sprouts
10 chives

Salt the skin side of the duck breasts and leave for 8 hours uncovered in the fridge to draw out the moisture. Wipe dry and rub in the five-spice powder.
Preheat the oven to 400°F. Fry the duck breasts in a dry frying pan over medium-high heat, skin side down, for 5 minutes.
Transfer the duck to a roasting pan and cook in the oven for 10 minutes, skin-side uppermost, until the skin is brown and crisp and the flesh is medium rare. Allow an extra 10 minutes for well done. Remove from the oven and cool.
Split each duck breast in half, then cut them crosswise into thin strips. Toss the duck in the hoisin sauce.
Divide the duck, scallions, cucumber, and bean sprouts among the pancakes. Roll up and tie a chive around the middle, securing with a knot. Serve.

Advance preparation: Cook the duck and prepare the scallions and cucumber 8 hours ahead, cover, and chill. Assemble 1 hour before serving.
Freezing: Not suitable.

right Crispy duck pancakes

Radishes with watercress butter

Any spare watercress butter can be used for filling tiny baked potatoes, in sandwiches (the pepperiness helps the flavor of cucumber no end), or piped onto Parmesan Toasts (page 54). MAKES 20

10 radishes, halved lengthwise
for the watercress butter
4 tblsp unsalted butter, softened
1 cup watercress leaves
1 small clove garlic, crushed
Salt & freshly ground pepper to taste
You will also need a pastry bag and small plain pastry tip

Blend all the ingredients for the watercress butter in a blender or processor until smooth. Adjust the seasoning to taste.
Trim a thin slice from the base of each halved radish to keep them upright. Pipe or spoon the butter on top. Serve.

Radishes with watercress butter

Advance preparation: The radishes can be topped 4 hours in advance, covered, and chilled. Remove from the fridge 30 minutes before serving.
Freezing: The watercress butter can be frozen up to 4 weeks ahead.

Celery with olive & parsley salad

Gay Bilson's recipe from Stephanie Alexander's book Stephanie's Australia *was the source of the salad, which I have changed a little. She serves it as a first course with Parmesan shavings and some deep-fried water crackers. Over the years I have found myriad uses for it and often make a chunky version with anchovies and sun-dried tomatoes to scatter over sliced mozzarella (page 129).* MAKES 10

2 large stalks celery, cut diagonally into 5
for the olive & parsley salad
3 tblsp pitted black olives, chopped
1 heaping tblsp diced red onion
1 heaping tblsp chopped fresh parsley
1 tblsp capers, drained
2 tsp olive oil
1 small clove garlic, crushed
Freshly ground pepper to taste
A few curls of lemon zest to garnish

Toss all the ingredients together for the olive-parsley salad, except the lemon zest.
Spoon the salad into the celery lengths and garnish with the curls of zest.

Advance preparation: Crush the garlic and chop the olives, onion, and parsley; store separately, covered, in the fridge, up to 1 day before. Combine the salad and fill the celery up to 4 hours ahead.
Freezing: Not suitable.

Belgian endive with Roquefort, pecans & cranberries

These ingredients also make a good autumnal fork salad if you toss them in a walnut oil dressing. SERVES 10

1 head Belgian endive
1½ tblsp dried cranberries
2 tblsp pecans or walnuts, coarsely chopped
⅓ cup crumbled Roquefort cheese
A few sprigs of watercress

Trim the base of the endive using a diagonal cut, then separate the leaves.

Toss the cranberries, nuts, and Roquefort together in a bowl, being careful not to break up the Roquefort too much.
Spoon the mixture into the endive leaves and garnish with the watercress.

Advance preparation: Fill the belgian endive leaves up to 3 hours before, cover, and chill. Garnish just before serving.
Freezing: Not suitable.

Shrimp & cucumber hearts with sweet chili sauce

Slices of cucumber make neat containers for strongly flavored fillings, like Szechwan Chicken (page 59), Olive & Parsley Salad (left), lemony crab (page 33) and crispy vegetables (page 33). For weddings, a pretty and romantic touch is to stamp the cucumber into hearts. MAKES 10

1 English (hothouse) cucumber
1 scallion
20 small peeled cooked shrimp
2 tsp sweet chili sauce
A few curls of lemon zest
You will also need a 1½-inch heart-shaped or round cutter

Cut the cucumber into 10 diagonal slices ½ inch thick so they are wide enough to fit the cutter. Cut out shapes using the cutter, which will also remove the skin.
Place the cucumber on a plate lined with paper towels and lay some more paper on top to absorb the excess moisture. Leave for about 1 hour to dry.
Slice the scallion into 1¼-inch lengths and then again into long, fine strips. Put into a bowl of ice water for 1 hour so that the strips become curly. Dry on paper towels.
Arrange 2 shrimp on each cucumber heart, spoon over some chili sauce, and garnish with the scallion and zest.

Advance preparation: 12 hours before, cut the cucumber and place on paper; put the scallion strips in water. Cover both and chill. Fill 2 hours before.
Freezing: Not suitable.

Pesto, tapenade & sun-dried tomato potatoes

Bite-sized or man-sized, Mediterranean potatoes are always a hit, whether they are for drinks or supper parties. To make smooth versions of the pesto and tapenade, blend them thoroughly in a food processor or grind using a pestle and mortar. MAKES 30

30 small new red potatoes
2 tblsp grated Parmesan cheese
Salt & freshly ground pepper to taste

for the sun-dried tomato paste
3 tblsp coarsely chopped sun-dried
   tomatoes in oil, drained
½ tblsp sun-dried tomato oil reserved
   from the tomatoes, or olive oil
2 tblsp grated Parmesan cheese

for the chunky pesto
(makes ⅓ cup)
½ cup fresh basil or cilantro leaves
2½ tblsp pine nuts, toasted
1 small clove garlic, crushed
1 tblsp olive oil
¼ cup grated Parmesan cheese
Salt & freshly ground pepper to taste

for the chunky tapenade
(makes ⅓ cup)
¼ cup pitted black olives
2 heaping tblsp fresh parsley leaves
2 tblsp capers, drained
1 tsp Dijon mustard
1 tblsp olive oil
Freshly ground pepper to taste

Mix together all the ingredients for the sun-dried tomato paste.
Make the chunky pesto by chopping the basil or cilantro coarsely and placing it in a bowl with the pine nuts, garlic, olive oil, Parmesan and seasoning. Mix well.
Make the chunky tapenade by coarsely chopping the olives, parsley, and capers together. Place them in a bowl with the mustard, olive oil, and seasoning and stir.
Boil the potatoes for 5–8 minutes or until tender. Cut a lid from each and discard.
Hollow out the potatoes with a teaspoon and mash the flesh with a fork. Divide the flesh among 3 bowls.
Add the sun-dried tomato paste to one batch, the pesto to another, and the tapenade to the third. Mix each batch well

Celery with olive & parsley salad

with some seasoning.
Preheat the oven to 375°F. Separately fill the potato shells with the flavored mixtures, sprinkle with Parmesan, and bake them for 10 minutes or until golden brown and piping hot. Serve.

Advance preparation: Make the sun-dried tomato paste and tapenade up to 4 days before, cover, and chill. Normally, you would make a chunky pesto at the last minute, as the basil will discolor if

stored. However, since the basil will lose some of its color on baking, it is fine to make it up to 1 day before. If you are making a smooth pesto, it can be blended up to 4 days ahead and stored covered with a film of olive oil; pour off the oil before using. You can also cook and fill the potatoes up to 1 day ahead, then cover and chill. Reheat them for 15 minutes at 375°F.
Freezing: Not suitable.

Above: *The basic Cheddar cracker recipe can be used in many ways. Here it is topped with soft goat cheese, sliced tomatoes, and purple basil.* Right: *As an alternative to traditional wedding cake, a delicious heart-shaped chocolate Sachertorte topped with rose petals is a stunning choice and can double as dessert. Bake it in large or small cake pans and choose the petals to match the bouquet and decorations.*

the menu

Herbed brioche sandwiches

Shrimp & cucumber hearts with sweet chili sauce

Cheddar crackers with goat cheese, tomatoes & basil

Parmesan, arugula & salsa verde sandwiches

Elderflower jellies

Summer berry tartlets

Vanilla shortbreads with fromage frais & lime curd

Heart cake with rose petals

Jasmine infusion

wedding

Above: *It is a special occasion, so offer a welcoming nonalcoholic drink such as the Jasmine Infusion in the prettiest glasses you can find and serve them from a matching tray. Sugar swizzle sticks allow guests to sweeten the drinks to their taste and add a sense of fun.* **Right:** *Choose a variety of tiny perfect fruits for the tartlets and display them in rows of uniform color for maximum impact.*

Left: *These pretty sandwiches are also easy to make. Rounds of brioche are dipped in lemony mayonnaise, then rolled in herbs. Serve with Parmesan, Arugula and Salsa Verde Sandwiches cut into squares.* Below: *A choice of dessert canapés presented on platters chosen to suit the occasion — at a wedding, it is important that the serving dishes, glasses, and table decorations reflect the couple's sense of style.*

Left: *A heart-shaped cutter is all that is needed to turn slices of cucumber into a romantic party piece. Here, the cucumber base is topped with fresh shrimp and sweet chili sauce — there is no reason why wedding food should not have a contemporary flavor.* Above: *Light and cool, fruit jellies made from elderflower cordial and a variety of fresh berries appeal to guests of all ages.*

Hot dogs

For an Americana party, serve these hot dogs with mini hamburgers (right), Maryland crab cakes (page 51), and tiny Thanksgiving croustades (page 51). MAKES 10

1 small onion, finely sliced
2 tblsp butter
1 tblsp vegetable oil
10 mini hot dog buns
5 mini frankfurters, halved lengthwise
1 tblsp tomato ketchup
1 tblsp yellow mustard
Salt & freshly ground pepper to taste
You will also need 2 pastry bags and two ¼-inch plain pastry tips

Fry the onion in the butter and oil over low heat for about 20–30 minutes, stirring often, until soft and rich golden. Season.
Preheat the oven to 375°F. Split the hot dog buns and fill each with some of the onions and a frankfurter half. Transfer to a baking sheet and bake for 6–8 minutes or until hot.
Spoon the ketchup and the mustard separately into pastry bags fitted with pastry tips and pipe a squiggle of each onto the frankfurters. Serve.

Advance preparation: Cook the onions up to 2 days ahead, cover, and chill. Fill the hot dog rolls with the onions and frankfurters up to 3 hours before, cover, and chill. Bake to order.
Freezing: The onions can be cooked and frozen up to 4 weeks before.

Hamburgers

Hamburgers

In this recipe, Maryland crab cakes (page 51) can be substituted for the hamburger mixture if you prefer. The chili relish will taste great with both. MAKES 10

Vegetable oil for frying
10 mini hamburger buns, split in half
5 tsp chili relish
A few leaves of curly endive
for the hamburgers
7 oz ground beef
½ cup finely chopped shallots
2 tblsp Worcestershire sauce
1 tblsp tomato ketchup
Salt & freshly ground pepper to taste

Mix all the ingredients together for the burgers. Divide the mixture into 10 balls, flatten, and shape into burgers.
Fry in batches in hot oil for 2–3 minutes on each side or until cooked through.
Spread the base of the rolls with the relish, top with a few leaves of curly endive, then the burgers. Put the lids on top and serve.

Advance preparation: Mix and shape the burgers, cover, and refrigerate up to 3 hours ahead. Fry and fill to order.
Freezing: Not suitable.

Cheddar scones with mustard butter & ham

These Cheddar scones are the best ever! Boastful, I know, but true. As with all scone mixtures, try to handle the dough as little as possible for a light result. If you are able, bake and serve them straight from the oven, filled or unfilled. MAKES 10

2 tblsp unsalted butter, softened
1 heaping tsp coarse-grained mustard
2½oz wafer-thin ham, cut into 10 slices
Salt & freshly ground pepper to taste
for the Cheddar scones
1 cup all-purpose flour, sifted + extra for rolling
1 slightly heaping tsp baking powder
½ tsp sugar
A large pinch of salt
⅔ cup heavy cream

¼ cup milk

heaping ⅓ cup mature shredded Cheddar
  cheese

1 tblsp melted unsalted butter
  + extra for greasing

You will also need a 1½in-round cutter

Mix the flour, baking powder, sugar and
salt together in a bowl. Add the cream,
milk and ¼ cup of the cheese and gently
mix together just enough to combine into
a soft dough.

Turn out the dough onto a floured surface
and knead very lightly, just once or twice,
to incorporate the cream and cheese.

Roll the dough out gently to a thickness
of ½in and stamp out the scones.
Reroll and stamp out any trimmings,
remembering they will not be as light as
the first batch, nor will they rise as evenly.

Preheat the oven to 400°F. Transfer the
scones to a greased baking sheet and set
aside for 10 minutes to rest.

Brush the tops of the scones with the
melted butter and sprinkle with the
remaining cheese.

Bake the scones for about 10 minutes in
the hot oven or until well risen and
golden.

Remove to a wire rack to cool if filling;
otherwise, serve straight from the oven.

Mix the softened butter, mustard, and
seasoning together and divide the mixture
among the split scones. Add a piece of
ham to each scone and serve.

Advance preparation: Bake the scones
up to 8 hours before and store in an airtight container. Fill 1 hour before serving,
cover, and keep cool.

*Freezing: Freeze the unbaked scones up
to 2 weeks before; bake straight from the
freezer in a preheated 375°F oven for 15
minutes. Baked scones can be frozen up
to 3 weeks ahead and reheated at 350°F.*

left Hot dogs

Bacon & egg croustades

These miniature versions of a traditional cooked breakfast are simple to make, but they never fail to please and amuse guests. I often serve them to kick off brunches, or to end late-night cocktail parties. MAKES 12

4 thin slices white bread, crusts removed
2 tblsp butter, melted + extra for greasing
2 thick slices bacon
12 small wild mushrooms, or 3 small
  white mushrooms, quartered
1 tblsp butter
12 quail eggs
3 very small cherry tomatoes, quartered
Salt & freshly ground pepper to taste
You will also need a set of 12 round tartlet pans 1½ inches in diameter

Preheat the oven to 375°F. Roll the bread out thinly with a rolling pin and cut each slice into 4 quarters.
Grease the tartlet pans and line them with the bread, pressing it down into the bottom and up the sides of the pans, to make a four-cornered shell.
Brush the shell well with the melted butter and bake for 7–10 minutes or until golden brown. Remove from the pans to a baking sheet (if making the canapés all at once, leave the oven on).
Broil or panfry the bacon for 2–3 minutes or until crisp. Drain on paper towels, then cut into 12 pieces.
Sauté the mushrooms in the butter over a medium heat for 3–4 minutes or until cooked. Season and drain on paper towels.
Crack open the quail eggs and carefully slip 1 into each of the croustades. Divide the bacon, mushrooms, and cherry tomatoes among them and season.
Bake for 5–7 minutes or until the whites of the quail eggs are set and the rest of the ingredients are piping hot. Serve.

Advance preparation: Fill the croustades up to 2 hours before, cover, and chill. Bake to order.
Freezing: The cooked croustades, bacon, and mushrooms can be frozen up to 4 weeks ahead.

Sausage & mash croustades

If you are ever making mashed potatoes for another recipe, save some and freeze it for use in this, as it's such a tiny amount to have to make otherwise. You could also use my parsley mash recipe (page 36). MAKES 12

One 4-oz boiling potato, quartered
2 tblsp butter
3 chipolata sausages
Vegetable oil for roasting
2 shallots, sliced into rings
12 croustades (see Bacon & Egg
  Croustades Recipe, left)
2 tsp tomato ketchup

Cook the potato in a pan of salted water for 15–20 minutes or until tender. Drain and purée while still hot, using a food mill, ricer, or sieve (using a food processor will make the potato gluey). Add half the butter, season, and mix well.
Preheat the oven to 375°F. Cook the sausages in a little oil in the oven for 10–15 minutes or until golden brown. Drain on paper towels and slice each sausage diagonally into 8.
Fry the shallots in the remaining butter over medium heat for 5 minutes or until crisp and golden. Drain on paper towels.
Fill each of the croustades with some potato purée, 2 slices of sausage, and a few shallot rings.
Warm the croustades through in the hot oven for 5–8 minutes. Spoon on some ketchup before serving.

Advance preparation: Fill the croustades up to 2 hours before, cover, and chill. Bake to order.
Freezing: The cooked croustades, mashed potato, and shallots can be frozen up to 4 weeks before.

Miniature British Christmas dinners

Although everyone loves these Lilliputian Christmas dinners in a bite, they do take time to make. The bread sauce is a short-cut version that I have developed since it is such a tiny amount to prepare. But if you want to make the real thing, do so. MAKES 12

3 Brussels sprouts
1½ tblsp fresh bread crumbs
1½ tblsp whole milk
A small pinch of ground nutmeg
A small piece of butter
1 thick slice bacon
12 croustades (see Bacon & Egg
  Croustades Recipe, left)
3oz cooked turkey breast, cut into 12
  pieces
24 pieces broken potato chips
3 tblsp chicken or turkey gravy
Salt & freshly ground pepper to taste

Boil the Brussels sprouts in a pan of salted water for 7–8 minutes or until tender. Drain, refresh in cold water, dry on paper towels, and then cut each sprout into 4 even pieces.
Make the bread sauce by soaking the crumbs in the milk for 5 minutes. Heat over low heat for 2–3 minutes. Add the nutmeg, seasoning, and the butter to make a spoonable consistency. Stir well and remove from the heat to cool.
Cook the bacon under the broiler or panfry for 2–3 minutes or until crisp. Drain on paper towels and then cut the bacon into 12 pieces. Cool.
Preheat the oven to 375°F. Fill the prepared croustades with a piece of turkey, Brussels sprout, bacon, and some crisps. Spoon on the bread sauce.
Place the filled croustades on a baking sheet and heat through in the oven for 5–8 minutes or until hot. Heat the gravy separately in a saucepan and spoon it over the croustades before serving.

Advance preparation: Fill the croustades, except for the gravy, up to 2 hours before, cover, and chill. Bake to order.
Freezing: The cooked croustades can be frozen up to 4 weeks before.

Vegetable oil for frying

Salt & freshly ground pepper to taste

12 cilantro leaves

for the cornmeal muffins

⅓ cup all-purpose flour

6 tblsp yellow cornmeal

1 tsp baking powder

A pinch of salt

2 tblsp butter, melted + extra for greasing

1 small egg, lightly beaten

3 tblsp milk

1 tsp finely chopped red bird's-eye chili

1 tblsp chopped fresh cilantro

for the Maryland crab cakes

2½ oz fresh lump crabmeat

3 tblsp fresh bread crumbs

1 tsp finely chopped red bird's-eye chili

1 tblsp chopped fresh cilantro

3 tblsp mayonnaise

1 small egg, lightly beaten

You will also need a mini muffin pan with 12 cups

Preheat the oven to 350°F. Prepare the muffins by sifting the flour, cornmeal, baking powder, and salt together into a bowl. Make a well in the center and quickly stir in the butter, egg, milk, chili, and cilantro. Mix well.

Grease the muffin cups and then divide the muffin mixture among them.

Bake the muffins for 10–12 minutes or until risen and golden. Transfer to a wire rack to cool and then split in half.

Mix all the ingredients for the crab cakes together and season well. Divide the mixture into 12 balls, then flatten and shape them into little cakes.

Fry the crab cakes in batches in hot oil for 1 minute on either side or until cooked. Remove them from the heat and quickly drain on paper towels.

Fill each of the muffins with a hot crab cake and a cilantro leaf and serve.

Advance preparation: Make the muffins up to 8 hours before and store in an airtight container. Mix and shape the crab cakes, chill, and cover up to 4 hours ahead. Fry and fill to order.

Freezing: Make the muffins and freeze up to 3 weeks before. Heat the muffins in a preheated 350°F oven for 3-4 minutes to freshen, then cool.

Cornmeal muffins with Maryland crab cakes

Miniature Thanksgiving dinners

Another recipe requiring nimble fingers: a bite-sized taste of Thanksgiving. MAKES 12

One 3-oz piece sweet potato, peeled and quartered

A small piece of butter

2 fresh ears baby corn, or bottled baby corn

12 croustades (see Bacon & Egg Croustades Recipe, page 50)

3 oz cooked turkey breast, cut into 12 pieces

3 tblsp chicken or turkey gravy

2 heaping tsp cranberry sauce

Salt & freshly ground pepper to taste

Cook the sweet potato in a pan of salted water for 15–20 minutes until tender. Drain, pass through a sieve, stir in the butter and seasoning, and allow to cool.

Boil the baby corn in a pan of salted water for 2–3 minutes or until tender. Drain, refresh in cold water, and dry on paper towels. Or use bottled corn. Cut each ear into 12 rounds.

Preheat the oven to 375°F. Fill the croustades with some sweet potato purée, a piece of turkey, and 2 slices of corn, then bake for 5–8 minutes or until hot.

Warm the gravy in a saucepan and divide it among the filled croustades. Top with the cranberry sauce just before serving.

Advance preparation: Fill the croustades, except for the gravy, up to 2 hours before; cover and chill. Bake to order.

Freezing: The cooked croustades and the sweet potato purée can be frozen up to 4 weeks before.

Cornmeal muffins with Maryland crab cakes

These buttery yellow cornmeal muffins, flecked with chili and cilantro, can be served unfilled straight from the oven if you like. Tapenade and chunky guacamole are good alternative fillings. MAKES 12

Brioches filled with wild mushrooms or scrambled eggs & caviar

If your budget does not stretch to caviar, as in this recipe, use some finely chopped smoked salmon and snipped chives with the eggs instead. A small nugget of foie gras slipped into the hollowed-out brioche and warmed through also makes a sublime, albeit pricey, filling, but chopped smoked ham and sautéed leeks stirred in a thick cheesy sauce is equally good. MAKES 20

20 bite-sized brioches or savory muffins
for the wild mushroom filling
5 oz small wild mushooms
1 tblsp unsalted butter
1 tblsp olive oil
½ small clove garlic, crushed
A large pinch of fresh thyme leaves
Salt & freshly ground pepper to taste
for the scrambled eggs & caviar filling
2 medium eggs, lightly beaten
1 tblsp unsalted butter
1 tblsp heavy cream
2 oz sevruga caviar
Salt & freshly ground pepper to taste

Cut the tops off the brioches, reserving the lids. Hollow out the brioches using a small sharp knife or melon baller.
Sauté the mushrooms in the butter, olive oil, and garlic over medium heat until cooked, about 3–4 minutes. Stir in the thyme and seasoning and let cool.
Spoon the mushroom mixture into 10 of the brioches and put the lids on top.
Preheat the oven to 350°F. Put the filled and the unfilled brioches separately on baking sheets and cover loosely with foil. Warm the filled brioches in the oven for 10–12 minutes and the unfilled brioches for 2–3 minutes only.
Pass the eggs through a sieve. Melt the butter in a small, heavy pan over very low heat, add the eggs, and stir constantly for 2–3 minutes or until the eggs are creamy and just hold their shape.
Remove from the heat. Stir in the cream, season, then transfer the eggs to a bowl.

left Saffron mussels in garlic bread

Spoon the eggs into the warm brioches, top with the caviar and the lids, and serve alongside the mushroom brioches.

Advance preparation: Up to 4 hours before, hollow out all the brioches, cover, and set 10 of them aside. Fill the rest with the cold sautéed mushrooms, cover, and chill. Warm the filled brioches in a preheated 350°F oven for 5-7 minutes. Fill the others to order.
Freezing: Not suitable.

Camembert ice cream on Parmesan toasts

Camembert ice cream, accompanied with Parmesan toasts, is an unusual canapé but also makes a fabulous cheese course at lunch or supper. My basic recipe is taken from Jane Grigson's book Good Things. *She liked to serve it with heated water biscuits, and quite delicious it is too.* MAKES 10

10 Parmesan Toasts (page 54)
A few small salad leaves, such as arugula
   or mustard greens
for the Camembert ice cream
4 oz ripe Camembert or Brie, rind trimmed
4 tblsp half-and-half
4 tblsp heavy cream
Tabasco sauce or cayenne pepper
   and salt to taste

Blend the cheese and half-and-half together in a blender or processor for about 30 seconds or until smooth. Stir in the cream and season well with Tabasco or cayenne and salt.
Transfer the mixture to a lidded plastic container and freeze for about 3–4 hours or until firm (there is no need to stir it).
Unmold the ice cream onto a board, cut off small shavings with a sharp knife, and arrange on the Parmesan toasts.
Garnish each of the canapés with a single salad leaf and serve.

Advance preparation: Top the Parmesan toasts with the ice cream just 5 minutes before serving.
Freezing: Make and freeze the ice cream up to 2 weeks in advance.

Saffron mussels in garlic bread

Garlic, saffron, and mussels: a marriage made in heaven. MAKES 10

Ten 1-inch slices small baguette
1 clove garlic
for the saffron mussels
2 shallots, finely chopped
1 small clove garlic, crushed
2 tblsp butter
¼ cup dry white wine
7 oz small fresh mussels
⅔ cup heavy cream
5–6 saffron threads
1 tblsp chopped fresh parsley
Salt & freshly ground pepper to taste

Preheat the oven to 375°F. Scoop some of the bread out of the centre of the baguette slices. Rub the bread all over with the garlic. Bake for 5–8 minutes or until just colored and slightly crisp.
Cook the shallots in the butter in a large pan over medium heat for 5 minutes until softened.
Pour in the wine, increase the heat to high, stir well, and then add the mussels. Cover and steam for 4–5 minutes or until all the shells have opened. Discard any that remain unopened.
Lift out the mussels with a slotted spoon and cool before removing the meat from the shells. Strain and reserve the liquid.
Set the oven to 350°F. Put the baguette slices into the oven to warm through for 1–2 minutes.
Stir the cream, saffron, and parsley into the mussel juices and, if necessary, reduce the liquid by boiling it to a coating consistency. Season to taste.
Return the mussel meat to the pan and heat through for 1–2 minutes over medium heat. Spoon the mussels and sauce onto the warm bread and serve.

Advance preparation: Combine the mussels and sauce 6 hours before, cover, and chill. Heat over medium heat for 4–5 minutes or until very hot. Fill the warmed baguette slices to order.
Freezing: The baked baguette slices can be frozen up to 4 weeks ahead.

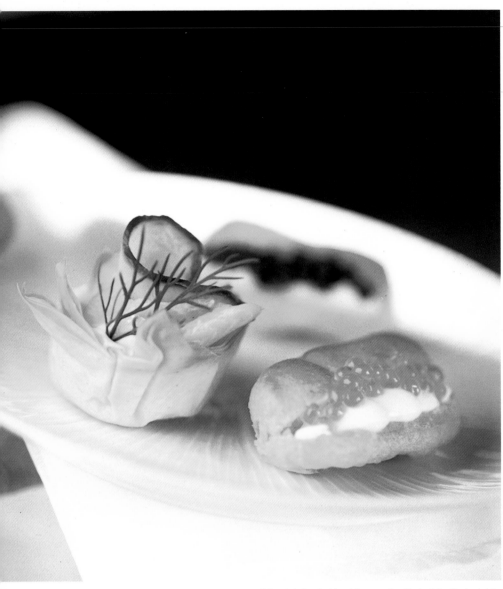

Preheat the oven to 375°F. Bake the straws for 8–10 minutes or until golden brown. Transfer to a wire rack to cool. Serve warm or cold.

Advance preparation: Bake the straws 4 days before and store in an airtight container. Heat through in a preheated 350°F oven for 3-4 minutes to crisp. *Freezing: Freeze the straws unbaked up to 4 weeks before and bake frozen, or freeze them baked 3 weeks ahead and heat through as above.*

Parmesan toasts

These cheesy toasts are an updated version of melba toast and a good way to use up any bread that is past its best. Serve them at cocktail parties when you want something very simple among more complicated canapés, or top with Camembert Ice Cream (page 53). At stand-up fork buffets, Parmesan toasts are an extremely practical bread to serve as they do not require any butter and therefore no knives MAKES 20

20 very thin slices bread, such as
   ciabatta, focaccia, or baguette
4 tblsp butter, melted, or olive oil
3 tblsp finely grated Parmesan
Salt & freshly ground pepper to taste

Preheat the oven to 375°F. Divide the sliced bread among some baking sheets and brush the upper sides of the bread with the melted butter. Liberally sprinkle with the Parmesan and season well with salt and pepper.
Bake the toasts on two shelves in the oven for 8–12 minutes or until crisp and golden, switching the trays halfway through cooking. Cool before serving.

Advance preparation: Make the toasts up to 1 week in advance and store in an airtight container. Warm through in a preheated 350°F oven for 2-3 minutes to crisp.
Freezing: Make and freeze up to 4 weeks ahead. Heat through as above.

left to right Smoked trout & cucumber filo tartlets, Caviar éclairs

Sesame cheese straws

When friends are coming over for a quick drink, I like to serve these with a mixture of other simple nibbles, such as Parmesan toasts and anchovy pastries. They can all be pulled out of the freezer and quickly warmed through to freshen them up. MAKES 30

7 tblsp unsalted butter + extra
   for greasing
1 cup all-purpose flour + extra for rolling
1 cup shredded cheddar cheese
½ tsp cayenne pepper
A large pinch of salt
2 tsp sesame seeds
You will also need a fluted pasta wheel

Mix the butter and flour together in a food processor for 30 seconds or until they resemble fine bread crumbs. Add the cheese, cayenne, and salt and pulse 4–5 times or just until a dough forms.
Transfer to a lightly floured surface and knead the pastry for 1 minute. Wrap in plastic wrap and chill for 30 minutes.
Roll out the dough to a thickness of ¼ inch on a lightly floured surface and then, using a fluted pasta wheel, cut the pastry into straws about 6 inches long and ½ inch wide. Reroll the trimmings to the same thickness and cut to make a total of 30 straws.
Sprinkle the pastries with sesame seeds, then place them on lightly greased baking sheets. Chill for 30 minutes.

Anchovy pastries

If, like me, you love salty foods, anchovy pastries fit the bill nicely. MAKES 10

1 sheet frozen puff pastry, thawed
Flour for rolling
5 salted anchovies, rinsed & drained
1 tsp butter, melted

Roll out the pastry very thinly on a lightly floured surface and cut into an 8-inch square. Cut the pastry square in half.
Lay the anchovies, one beneath the other, across the width of one piece of pastry, leaving a gap between each anchovy.
Brush the remaining piece of pastry with water, turn it over, and lift it onto the anchovy-topped pastry. Press down firmly between each anchovy and brush all over with melted butter.
Cut down the length of the pastry, through the anchovies, to make 10 equal strips. Transfer the pastries to a lightly greased baking sheet and chill for 30 minutes.
Preheat the oven to 375°F. Bake the pastries for 8 minutes or until golden. Serve warm or cold.

Advance preparation: Bake up to 1 day before, store in an airtight container, and reheat in a preheated 350°F oven for 2–3 minutes to crisp.
Freezing: Freeze the pastries 3 weeks before and heat through as above.

Curry puffs

These Indian-style puff pastries are best served straight from the oven, as they become too dry if reheated. MAKES 10

1 sheet frozen puff pastry, thawed
4 tsp medium-hot curry paste
Butter for greasing
1 small egg yolk
1 tsp water
½ tsp salt
½ tsp cumin seeds
Flour for rolling
You will also need a 2-inch fluted cutter

Roll the pastry out on a lightly floured surface to a thickness of ⅛ inch and trim

to a rectangle 8 x 10 inches. Cut the pastry into three 8 x 3⅓-inch pieces.
Divide the curry paste between 2 of the pieces, spread the mixture to the edges, and stack the sheets on top of each other. Put the last piece on top and roll lightly to make a stack ¼ inch thick.
Cut out 10 rounds using the cutter. Place them on a lightly greased baking sheet, leaving a little space between each.
Mix the egg yolk, water, and salt together. Brush this over the tops of the pastries and sprinkle with the cumin. Do not let the egg drip over the sides, as this will stop the pastry from rising. Chill for 30 minutes.
Preheat the oven to 375°F and bake the puffs for 8–10 minutes or until they are well risen and golden. Serve hot.

Advance preparation: Make up to the stage of glazing, cover, and chill up to 1 day ahead. Glaze and bake as above.
Freezing: Freeze uncooked up to 4 weeks before. Bake as above.

Caviar éclairs

Who wants a chocolate éclair when you can have a caviar-filled éclair instead? Lumpfish roe is no substitute for real caviar, so do not even think about using it! MAKES 16

Choux pastry dough (page 81)
Butter for greasing
6 tblsp crème fraîche
1½ oz sevruga caviar
1½ oz salmon caviar
You will also need a pastry bag and plain ½-inch pastry tip

Preheat the oven to 400°F. Put the pastry into a pastry bag and pipe 2-inch lengths of pastry, well apart, onto a lightly greased baking sheet.
Bake the éclairs for 10–12 minutes or until golden. Make a slit in the side of each, return to the oven, and leave the door ajar for 5 minutes to dry out the pastry.
Cool the éclairs on a wire rack and then make a bigger slit in the sides.
Spoon the crème fraîche into a pastry bag fitted with a pastry tip and fill the éclairs.

Garnish half with the sevruga caviar and the rest with the salmon caviar. Serve.

Advance preparation: Make the éclairs up to 1 day in advance and store in an airtight container. Crisp them for 2–3 minutes in a preheated 350°F oven and let cool before filling. Fill up to 1 hour before serving.
Freezing: Freeze the baked pastries up to 3 weeks ahead, crisp, and fill as above.

Smoked trout & cucumber filo tartlets

Smoked eel, mackerel, or salmon can be used instead of trout in this recipe. MAKES 12

Three 12-inch square sheets filo pastry
2 tblsp butter, melted
3 tblsp crème fraîche
1 tsp prepared horseradish
4 oz smoked pink trout fillets, cut into 12
1-inch piece cucumber, halved, seeded & cut into 12 pieces
A few sprigs of dill
Freshly ground pepper to taste
You will also need a set of 12 round tartlet pans 1½ inches in diameter

Brush 2 of the sheets of pastry with half the melted butter, lay them on top of each other, and press the third unbuttered sheet on top. Cut into 12 equal squares.
Preheat the oven to 375°F. Grease the tartlet pans and line them with the pastry, making a four-cornered crust.
Bake for 7–10 minutes or until golden brown. Transfer to a wire rack to cool.
Mix the crème fraîche and horseradish together with some black pepper and spoon into the crusts. Arrange a piece of trout on top of each, then a cucumber slice and a sprig of dill. Serve.

Advance preparation: Mix the crème fraîche and horseradish and slice the cucumber 4 hours before; cover and chill. Fill the tarts up to 15 minutes before.
Freezing: Freeze the baked tart shells 3 weeks before. Reheat in a preheated 350°F oven for 3–4 minutes, then cool and fill.

Cheddar crackers, goat cheese, tomatoes & basil

I have a really wide range of toppings that I like to use for these versatile Cheddar crackers. They include mozzarella and salsa verde (page 64); pesto or tapenade (page 43); chargrilled asparagus and roasted cherry tomatoes; cream cheese and chutney; and also watercress butter (page 42). They are also terrific served plain. MAKES 12

⅓ recipe Sesame Cheese Straws dough
  (page 54), made without sesame seeds
Flour for dusting
Butter for greasing
2 oz goat cheese, softened
6 yellow or red cherry tomatoes, sliced
  into 4
A few purple or green basil leaves
You will also need a 1¼-inch plain cutter, a pastry bag and a small plain pastry tip

Roll the pastry out to a thickness of ¼ inch on a lightly floured surface and then cut out discs using the cutter. Reroll any trimmings and cut out again.

Place the pastry discs on lightly greased baking sheets and chill for 30 minutes.

Preheat the oven to 375°F. Bake the crackers for 8–10 minutes or until they are golden brown, then transfer them to a wire rack to cool.

Spoon the softened goat cheese into a pastry bag fitted with a nozzle and pipe a little onto each cracker.

Arrange 2 slices of tomato on top of each mound of goat cheese, then garnish each cracker with a basil leaf and serve.

Advance preparation: Bake the crackers up to 4 days before and store them in an airtight container. Reheat the crackers in a preheated 350°F oven to crisp, then allow them to cool before topping. Slice the tomatoes up to 4 hours ahead, cover, and chill. Top the crackers 20 minutes before serving.

Freezing: Freeze the crackers unbaked up to 4 weeks before and bake from frozen, or freeze baked up to 3 weeks ahead and warm through as above.

Red onion, goat cheese & zucchini pastries

I often make larger versions of these pizza-like pastries, cutting them into 5½-inch rounds, to serve as a first course or lunch dish with salad. Do not hesitate to try different toppings, substituting roasted tomatoes for the zucchinis and feta or mozzarella for the goat cheese. MAKES 10

5 oz puff pastry
Flour for dusting
1 tblsp butter
½ tsp sugar
½ small red onion, sliced into wedges
  through the root
1 tsp red wine vinegar
1 very small zucchini, thinly sliced
  into rounds
⅓ cup crumbled goat cheese
1 tblsp olive oil
2 tsp thyme leaves
Salt & freshly ground pepper to taste
You will also need some parchment paper

Roll the pastry out on a lightly floured surface to a 2 x 15-inch strip. Then cut the pastry into Ten 2 x 1½-inch strips.

Place the pastry strips on a baking sheet lined with parchment paper and chill them for 30 minutes.

Melt the butter and sugar together in a frying pan over low heat, add the onion and cook for 5–8 minutes or until softened. Add the vinegar and let cool.

Preheat the oven to 400°F. Arrange the onion and zucchini on top of the pastries. Crumble the goat cheese over the top and drizzle with the oil. Scatter with the thyme and season thoroughly with salt and pepper.

Bake the pastries for 8 minutes or until well risen and golden. Serve hot.

Advance preparation: Assemble the pastries up to the point of baking and chill, covered, up to 6 hours in advance. Bake as above.

Freezing: Freeze the pastries ready to bake. Cook frozen, allowing about 10 minutes in the oven.

Mediterranean puffs

When time is short, this is a recipe where you can buy all the basics ready to do a quick assembly-line job. Good puff pastry, pesto, and tapenade are all readily available from supermarkets these days to make our lives easier in the kitchen. MAKES 30

14 oz puff pastry
Flour for dusting
Butter for greasing
1 small egg yolk
1 tsp water
½ tsp salt
2 tsp poppy seeds
2 tsp yellow mustard seeds
Chunky Pesto recipe (page 43), or
  ⅓ cup ready-made pesto
Chunky Tapenade recipe (page 43), or
  ⅓ cup ready-made tapenade
⅓ cup sun-dried tomatoes in oil, drained
  and coarsely chopped
¾ cup grated Parmesan cheese
¾ cup shredded Cheddar cheese
You will also need a 2-inch fluted cutter

Roll the pastry out on a lightly floured surface into a 12 x 14½-inch rectangle.

Cut out 30 pastry rounds using the cutter. Place them onto lightly greased baking sheets, leaving space between each to allow them to rise. Do not reroll the scraps as they will not rise evenly.

Mix the egg yolk, water, and salt together in a small bowl, then brush the tops of the pastries with this glaze. Do not let the glaze run over the sides of the pastries, as this will keep them from rising.

Sprinkle the pastries with the poppy and mustard seeds and chill for 30 minutes.

Preheat the oven to 375°F. Bake the pastries for 10–15 minutes or until they are well risen and a rich golden color. Cool on a wire rack.

Put the pesto, tapenade, and sun-dried tomatoes into 3 separate bowls, divide the Parmesan and Cheddar between them, and then separately pulse each batch in a blender until you have a thickish paste.

Split the cooked pastries in half. Spoon each of the fillings into 10 of the pastries and cover with the tops.

Mediterranean puffs

Place on baking sheets and reheat the pastries at 375°F for 10 minutes or until hot. Serve.

Advance preparation: Cut out the pastries, cover, and refrigerate up to 1 day ahead. On the day, glaze, bake, and fill up to 6 hours before. Reheat to order. *Freezing: Freeze either uncooked and unfilled up to 4 weeks before, or cooked and unfilled up to 3 weeks before.*

Quail egg & smoked salmon tartlets

Hollandaise sauce, eggs, and smoked salmon are made for each other. This canapé combines them cleverly in a bite-sized treat suitable for sophisticated brunches or cocktail parties. The versatile pastry recipe is used on several other occasions in this book. It will yield 1¼ lb pastry, which in turn will make: one hundred 1½-inch tartlets; eighteen 4-inch shallow tarts; or two 10-inch shallow tarts. Make the full quantity of pastry and freeze it in batches for other occasions. MAKES 12

6 quail eggs
2½ oz smoked salmon, cut into 12 pieces
A few sprigs of chervil
for the savory pastry
(makes 1¼ lb)
3 cups all-purpose flour, sifted + extra for dusting
A pinch of salt
1 cup (2 sticks) unsalted butter, diced
1 large egg, beaten
1 tblsp cold water
for the hollandaise sauce
4 tblsp unsalted butter
1 medium egg yolk
1 tblsp fresh lemon juice
Salt & freshly ground white pepper to taste
You will also need twelve 1½-inch round tartlet pans and a 2-inch plain cutter

Put the flour, salt, and butter together in a food processor and pulse 7–8 times or until the mixture resembles fine bread crumbs.

Turn into a bowl, add the egg and water, and mix to a dough. Knead well until smooth.

Wrap one eighth of the pastry in plastic wrap and chill for 30 minutes before using; freeze the remainder in batches for use in other recipes.

Roll out the chilled pastry thinly on a lightly floured surface and cut out 12 rounds with the cutter.

Line the tartlet pans, pressing the pastry down into the bottom and up the sides of the pans. Trim away any excess pastry, lightly prick the bases with a fork, and chill for 30 minutes.

Preheat the oven to 375°F. Bake the tartlets for 10 minutes or until golden. Cool them for 10 minutes before transferring from the pans to a baking sheet.

Put the quail eggs in a pan of water, bring to a boil, and cook for 3 minutes. Drain and leave under running cold water until cold. Shell, rinse away any shell, and dry on paper towels. Cut the eggs in half lengthwise.

Make the hollandaise sauce by first melting the unsalted butter in a small pan over a low heat and discarding any froth on the surface of the liquid.

Whisk the egg yolk with a dash of cold water over very low heat until thickened. Then, whisk in the melted butter, little by little, leaving behind any sediment in the bottom of the pan.

Stir the lemon juice and salt and pepper into the sauce and adjust the seasoning to taste. Remove the hollandaise from the heat and keep it warm by setting the pan over another pan of warm water.

Preheat the oven to 350°F. Fill each tartlet shell with a piece of salmon and half a quail egg. Cover loosely with foil and bake for 4–5 minutes or until warm, but not so hot that the salmon cooks.

Spoon some hollandaise sauce over each tartlet, garnish with chervil, and serve.

Advance preparation: Bake the tartlet shells up to 1 day before and store in an airtight container. Fill with the salmon and eggs up to 2 hours ahead, cover, and chill. Bake to order, then top with sauce. *Freezing: The tartlet shells can be frozen unbaked in their pans for up to 1 week and baked straight from the freezer. Freeze them baked up to 3 weeks ahead.*

Mixed bruschetta platter

The great thing about bruschetta is that they can be topped with virtually any type of food and they are an excellent way of using up leftovers. Bruschetta can even be sweet, made with fruit, as you will see later in the book (page 78). Serve this platter at parties where you want finger foods that are more substantial than the usual canapés. You can also choose just one of the bruschetta (this recipe makes 10 of each) to serve as part of a themed menu. Although bruschetta originated in Italy, do not feel restricted to Italian ingredients: The recipes here take inspiration from around the world. MAKES 50

Fifty ½-inch slices coarse-textured
   bread such as pugliese or sourdough
5 large cloves garlic
Olive oil for drizzling
Salt & freshly ground pepper to taste
for the asparagus, prosciutto & Parmesan bruschetta
15 asparagus spears, trimmed to
   4 inches and halved lengthwise
10 slices prosciutto di Parma
2 oz Parmesan cheese, shaved
for the tomato, bocconcini & basil bruschetta
10 Roma (plum) tomatoes, coarsely
   chopped
10 bocconcini cheeses (tiny mozzarella),
   each cut into 3, or 2 buffalo mozzarella,
   each cut into 5
2 tblsp torn basil leaves
for the sausage & mustard bruschetta
6 tblsp onion chutney or tomato relish
10 cooked spicy pork sausages, sliced
   diagonally into 4
2 tblsp mustard
A few sprigs of flat-leaf parsley
for the Szechwan chicken bruschetta
1¼ lb cooked chicken, shredded
Peanut Sauce (page 39)
¼ English (hothouse) cucumber,
   quartered lengthwise, seeded & cut
   into thin diagonal slices
2 scallions, thinly sliced
1 large hot red chili, thinly sliced
1 heaping tsp toasted sesame seeds

for the seafood bruschetta
¼ cup olive oil
1 tblsp fresh lemon juice
1 small clove garlic, crushed
8 oz small cooked squid rings
8 oz cooked shelled mussels
8 oz cooked peeled shrimp
A few sprigs of dill
*You will also need a pastry bag and
¼-inch plain pastry tip*

Toast the bread on both sides until crisp under a broiler or in a very hot ridged cast-iron grill pan. Rub the toasted bread with the garlic, pepper lightly, and drizzle with some olive oil. Cool.
Put the asparagus on a lightly oiled hot ridged cast-iron grill-pan and cook for 4–5 minutes, turning occasionally. Cool.
Divide the prosciutto and asparagus among 10 of the bruschetta and place a few Parmesan shavings on top.
Pile the tomatoes and bocconcini onto

10 bruschetta and scatter over the basil.
Spread the chutney or relish onto 10 bruschetta and place the sausages on top. Put the mustard into a pastry bag and pipe it over the sausages. Garnish with a sprig of parsley.
Arrange the chicken on 10 bruschetta, spoon over the peanut sauce, top with the cucumber and scallions and scatter over the chili and sesame seeds.
Mix the oil, lemon juice, garlic, and seasoning together for the seafood bruschetta and toss the shellfish in this dressing. Spoon onto the rest of the bruschetta and garnish with sprigs of dill.
Arrange on a platter and serve.

Advance preparation: Prepare the toppings 6 hours ahead, cover, and chill separately. Make the bruschetta and top up to 1 hour ahead, cover, and keep cool. *Freezing: Not suitable.*

Mixed bruschetta platter

left Szechwan chicken bruschetta

Smoked salmon & mascarpone crumpet pizzas

Scrambled eggs, crispy bacon, and roasted tomatoes are a terrific brunch topping for toasted crumpets. You can also use crumpets for classic pizza toppings. Children, and adults, will adore them. MAKES 10

10 crumpets
¾ cup (6 oz) mascarpone
5 oz smoked salmon, cut into 10 pieces
4 oz salmon caviar
A few sprigs of mizuna & chervil
Freshly ground pepper to taste

Toast the crumpets on both sides under the broiler for about 1 minute on either side or until golden.

Spread with the mascarpone while still hot, then arrange the smoked salmon on top and grind over some black pepper.

Spoon on the caviar and put a few herb leaves on top. Serve hot.

Advance preparation: Cut the salmon up to 4 hours before, cover, and chill.
Freezing: Not suitable.

Potato, garlic & rosemary pizzas

This is a great combination of ingredients: a crisp pizza base and tender potato with lots of garlic and rosemary. Crumbled grilled pancetta strewn on top of the potato tastes fantastic too. The yeastless pizza dough recipe, which is very quick to make, is taken from Lindsey Bareham's definitive book, In Praise of the Potato. MAKES 10

for the pizza base
2 cups all-purpose flour + extra
  for dusting
1 tsp baking soda
1 tsp cream of tartar
⅔ cup milk mixed with 1 tblsp vinegar
  to sour
1 tsp salt
for the topping
1 lb waxy potatoes, very thinly sliced
⅓ cup olive oil
2 large cloves garlic, crushed

1½ tblsp finely chopped fresh rosemary
heaping ½ cup grated Parmesan cheese
Sea salt & freshly ground pepper to taste

Sift the flour, baking soda, cream of tartar, and salt into a bowl. Using a wooden spoon, gradually mix in the milk, which has been soured with the vinegar, to make a soft dough. Put the dough on a floured surface, knead lightly, and then divide into 10 portions.

Roll each piece of dough into a ball, flatten, and then roll them into 4½-inch circles. Transfer the pizza bases to lightly floured baking sheets.

Preheat the oven to 400°F. Toss the potato slices with the oil, rosemary, and garlic, then season.

Arrange the potato on the pizza bases in circles, slightly overlapping like a French apple tart. Sprinkle over the Parmesan.

Bake for 8–10 minutes or until the pizza bases are crisp and the potatoes are tender and golden brown. Serve hot.

Advance preparation: Bake the pizzas up to 4 hours before and cover. Reheat at 375°F for 4–5 minutes.
Freezing: Not suitable.

Parmesan polenta pizzas

My pizzas come in lots of different guises. Here is one where the base is not made of bread dough, but polenta that has been sliced, coated, and fried. I always think the blandness of polenta is much improved when a generous amount of Parmesan is added. The toppings here are classic pizza flavors; you could also use some sautéed wild mushrooms (page 111). MAKES 10

for the pizza bases
4 cups water
3 cups instant polenta
½ cup (1 stick) butter
2½ cups (10 oz) grated Parmesan cheese
for the coating
1 cup instant polenta
1 cup (4 oz) grated Parmesan cheese
2 medium eggs, lightly beaten
⅔ cup vegetable oil
for the topping

1 lb robiola cheese or soft goat
  cheese, sliced into 20
8 roasted or sun-dried tomato halves,
  sliced
10 salted anchovies, cut into thirds
1 rounded tblsp capers in balsamic
  vinegar, drained
Salt & freshly ground pepper to taste

Make the pizza bases by heating the water in a large pan until boiling. Stir in the polenta and cook for 2 minutes, stirring constantly, until thick.

Remove the polenta from the heat and stir in the butter, Parmesan, and lots of salt and pepper. Cool for 10 minutes.

Take a large piece of plastic wrap about 12 x 16 inches wide. Spoon the cooked polenta down the center, fold the plastic wrap over it, and use this to help you shape the polenta into a smooth cylinder about 8 inches long and 4 inches wide. Chill for 1 hour.

Mix together the polenta and Parmesan for the coating. Cut the chilled cooked polenta into 10 even rounds. Coat them in the beaten egg and then in the polenta-Parmesan mixture.

Heat the oil in a skillet and fry the polenta in batches for 2–3 minutes on each side or until crisp. Drain on paper towels.

Put 2 slices of cheese on each polenta pizza and divide the tomatoes, anchovies, and capers amongst them.

Broil the pizzas for 3–4 minutes or until the cheese has melted and the polenta is hot. Serve immediately.

Advance preparation: Make the polenta up to 3 days before and chill. Coat and fry the bases up to 4 hours before; cool, top, cover, and chill. Broil to order.
Freezing: Not suitable.

right Parmesan polenta pizzas

Waffles with radish & cucumber cream cheese

Don't worry if you don't have a waffle iron, as you can cook spoonfuls of the batter in a heavy frying pan instead. MAKES 10

for the waffles
½ cup finely sliced scallions
1 tblsp butter + extra for
 greasing
½ cup self-rising flour, sifted
2 tblsp grated Parmesan cheese
¼ cup shredded Cheddar cheese
½ cup milk
1 egg, lightly beaten
for the radish & cucumber cream cheese
1⅓ cups coarsely grated cucumber
½ cup coarsely grated radishes
1 cup (4 oz) natural cream cheese
 or quark
1 heaping tblsp chopped fresh mint
 + extra mint leaves to garnish
Salt & freshly ground pepper to taste

Cook the scallions in the butter over a low heat for 2–3 minutes or until soft. Transfer to a large bowl and let cool.
Add the flour and cheeses to the scallions and make a well in the center. Pour in the milk, egg, and seasoning and mix well to make a thick batter. Whisk for 30 seconds and then let the batter stand for 5 minutes before using.
Heat a waffle iron and lightly grease with butter. Pour in half the batter and cook the waffles for 2–3 minutes or until golden brown. Transfer to a wire rack to cool. Repeat with the remaining batter, then break the cooked waffles into sections. Alternatively, cook spoonfuls of the batter in a greased heavy frying pan for about 2 minutes on each side.
Reserve 1 tablespoon *each* of the grated cucumber and radish for garnishing. Mix the rest into the cream cheese or quark with the chopped mint and seasoning.
Divide the topping among the waffles. Garnish with the reserved cucumber and radish and a sprig of mint. Serve.
Advance preparation: Cook the waffles 12 hours before and store in an airtight

left Waffles with radish & cucumber cream cheese

container. Reheat at 350°F for 2–3 minutes and cool before using. Make the topping 1 hour before and top the waffles 30 minutes before serving. Cover and keep cool.

Freezing: Freeze the waffles up to 2 weeks before. Reheat and cool as above.

Salmon caviar blini

If you want to scale these tiny blini up in size to serve as a first course, this recipe will make 4. I sometimes serve 3 blini for each person, separately topped with Chunky Pesto (page 43), Olive & Parsley Salad (page 42), and this salmon caviar topping. MAKES 14–16

for the blini
One 4-oz boiling potato, quartered
1 egg, separated
1 tblsp heavy cream
1 heaping tblsp self-rising flour
Grated nutmeg, salt & freshly ground
  pepper to taste
Vegetable oil for greasing

for the topping
2 tblsp crème fraîche
2 oz salmon caviar
2 tsp diced red onion
1 tsp finely snipped fresh chives

Cook the quartered potato in a pan of salted water for 15–20 minutes or until tender. Drain and purée while still hot, using a food mill, ricer, or a sieve.
Mix the potato, egg yolk, cream, flour, and seasoning together to make a thick batter. Beat the egg white until stiff but not dry and fold it into the potato batter.
Grease the frying pan and place it over medium heat. Cook teaspoons of the batter for about 1 minute on each side until golden. Transfer to a wire rack to cool.
Spoon the crème fraîche onto the blini, top with the salmon caviar, and sprinkle over the red onion and chives. Serve.

Advance preparation: Make the blini, dice the onion, and snip the chives 1 day ahead. Cover and chill. Top the blini up to 2 hours ahead, cover, and chill.

Freezing: Freeze the blini 2 weeks before. Refresh at 350°F for 2–3 minutes. Cool before serving.

Spicy dal cakes with avocado relish

These crisp, spicy Indian lentil cakes are topped with a cooling avocado and tomato relish. MAKES 10

for the spicy dahl cakes
⅔ cup split red lentils
1 hot green chili, finely chopped
1 small clove garlic, crushed
1½ tsp finely grated fresh ginger
½ tsp asafoetida powder
½ tsp salt
Vegetable oil for frying
for the avocado relish
1 small Roma (plum) tomato, peeled,
  seeded & coarsely chopped
¼ avocado, peeled and coarsely chopped
2 scallions, thinly sliced
2 tsp fresh lemon juice
Salt & freshly ground pepper to taste

Cover the lentils with cold water and soak for 8 hours.
Drain the lentils and blend them in a blender or processor with the chili, garlic, ginger, asafoetida, and salt for about 1 minute to make a thick paste.
Divide the lentil mixture into 10, flatten, and shape into cakes. Fry the cakes in batches in hot oil over medium heat for 3–4 minutes on each side or until crisp and golden. Drain and cool on paper towels.
Mix the chopped tomato with the avocado, scallions, and lemon juice, adding salt and pepper to taste.
Spoon the relish on top of the dal cakes and serve.

Advance preparation: Make the dal cakes up to 12 hours before and store in an airtight container. Make the relish and top the dal cakes 1 hour before; cover.
Freezing: Freeze the dal cakes 2 weeks ahead. Refresh at 350°F for 2–3 minutes. Cool.

Corn fritters with grilled corn & red pepper relish

Corn fritters are very easy to make. The smoky flavor is achieved by searing the corn on a cast-iron grill pan. I find the relish very handy and also use it in a Thanksgiving sandwich (page 68). MAKES 15

for the corn fritters
1½ ears fresh corn
⅔ cup self-rising flour
1 egg, lightly beaten
¼ cup milk
1 tsp olive oil
2 tblsp chopped fresh cilantro
1 tsp finely diced hot red chili
3–4 tblsp vegetable oil for frying
for the grilled corn & red pepper relish
½ ear fresh corn
½ small red onion, finely diced
½ small red bell pepper, seeded and
  finely diced
2 tsp chopped fresh sage
1 tbslp fresh lime juice
1 tblsp olive oil
Salt & freshly ground pepper to taste

Grill the corn, for both the fritters and the relish, on a very hot ridged cast-iron grill pan for about 10 minutes, turning it often, until nicely charred. Let cool.
Slice the corn kernels off the cobs. Put two thirds of the kernels into one bowl and the rest into another.
Stir the ingredients for the relish into the smaller amount of corn and season.
Sift the flour for the fritters into a bowl. Make a well in the center. Stir in the egg, milk, and olive oil to make a thick batter. Add the remaining corn, cilantro, chili, and seasoning and mix well.
Fry small spoonfuls of the batter in a frying pan of hot oil over medium heat for 3-4 minutes on either side or until golden. Drain and cool on paper towels.
Top the fritters with the relish and serve.

Advance preparation: Make the corn relish and the corn fritters up to 1 day ahead, cover, and chill. Top the fritters with the relish up to 2 hours before, cover, and keep cool.
Freezing: Not suitable.

Herbed brioche sandwiches

This pretty sandwich is perfect for weddings, christenings, and dainty afternoon teas. You can squeeze a little lemon juice into store-bought mayonnaise to boost its flavor. MAKES 12

Four ¼-inch-thick slices brioche loaf
1 rounded tblsp lemon mayonnaise
1 tblsp finely snipped fresh chives
1 tblsp finely chopped fresh dill
1 tsp chive flowers or similar
You will also need a 2-inch plain cutter

Cut out 10 circles from the brioche but do not include the crust.
Spread a thin coat of mayonnaise on the edge of each circle of brioche, taking care not to get mayonnaise on the top surface.
Mix the herbs together and roll the coated edges of the brioche in this mixture.
Shake gently to remove any excess herbs, arrange on a plate, and serve.

Advance preparation: Make 2 hours before. Cover well with a clean, damp cloth and plastic wrap, and chill.
Freezing: Not suitable.

Curried lobster sandwich

I know that an open-face lobster sandwich is not everyone's idea of fast food, but if you have bought the lobster and the mayonnaise, this is a 10-minute recipe. MAKES 10

5 thick slices sourdough or rye bread
Heaping ⅓ cup mayonnaise
2½ tsp mild curry paste
1 lb cooked lobster meat, cubed
1½ oz mixed salad greens, such as
  mizuna, mustard greens, or red chard
Salt & freshly ground pepper to taste
You will also need a 3-inch round cutter

Stamp out 10 circles from the bread but do not include the crust.
Stir the mayonnaise, curry paste, and seasoning together and toss in the lobster. Mix carefully but well.
Divide the salad leaves among the bread and top with the lobster. Serve.

Advance preparation: Make the curry mayonnaise 2 days before, cover, and chill. Assemble the sandwich 30 minutes before serving, cover, and chill.
Freezing: Not suitable.

Parmesan, arugula & salsa verde sandwiches

I thought that since the ubiquitous Parmesan cheese and arugula salad is such a marvelous combination, I would make a sandwich from them, adding a generous dollop of bright green, peppery salsa verde. The sauce is also wonderful stirred into hot pasta or served as an accompaniment to ham. MAKES 12

3 tblsp unsalted butter, softened
6 thin slices white country bread, such as
  pugliese or sourdough, crust removed
3 oz Parmesan cheese, shaved
1 cup arugula leaves
for the salsa verde
1½ cups arugula leaves
⅓ cup fresh basil leaves
⅓ cup fresh flat-leaf parsley
1 tsp Dijon mustard
1 tsp capers, drained
1½ tblsp olive oil
Salt & freshly ground pepper to taste

Make the salsa verde by pulsing the arugula, basil, and parsley leaves together in a food processor 6–7 times or until coarsely chopped. Add the rest of the sauce ingredients and blend for 30 seconds to make a coarse paste.
Butter the bread on one side only. Divide the salsa verde among 3 slices and spread it to the edges.
Layer the Parmesan and arugula leaves on top and cover with the remaining bread. **Press** down lightly, cut each sandwich into 4 squares, and serve.

Advance preparation: Make the salsa verde up to 4 days ahead, cover with a film of olive oil, and chill. Pour off the oil before using. Make the sandwiches 2 hours before; cover with a clean, damp cloth and plastic wrap, and chill.
Freezing: Not suitable.

Toasted brioches with crème fraîche & caviar

Not strictly a sandwich, more an assembly of ingredients, this indulgent recipe is for those times when you are feeling particularly generous towards your friends. Simply lay out the ingredients and let everyone make their own. MAKES 10

⅔ cup crème fraîche
1 tblsp finely snipped fresh chives
4 oz sevruga caviar
Ten ½-inch slices brioche loaf

Mix the crème fraîche and chives together and place in a serving bowl. Spoon the caviar carefully into another bowl.
Cut the brioche into 2-inch squares. Place them on a baking sheet and lightly toast under the broiler for about 30 seconds on either side.
Arrange the warm brioche in stacks on a plate and serve with the chive-flavored crème fraîche and the caviar.

Advance preparation: Toast the brioche up to 30 minutes before, leave on the baking sheet, cool, and cover. Warm briefly under a broiler before serving.
Freezing: Not suitable.

Garlic shrimp baguettes

Hot crusty bread filled with garlicky shrimp: no one can resist them. Serve a bottle of Tabasco alongside for those who like shrimp with piquancy. MAKES 10

10 mini baguettes
Garlic Butter (page 39)
1½ tblsp fresh lemon juice
1¾ lb medium shrimp, cooked, shelled,
  and deveined
1 bottle Tabasco sauce

Cut a thin slice from the top of the baguettes and discard. Remove most of the crumb from inside.
Warm the garlic butter with the lemon juice and stir in the shrimp.
Preheat the oven to 350°F. Divide the garlicky shrimp among the baguettes, place on a baking sheet and bake for

10–15 minutes or until piping hot. Serve with a bottle of Tabasco sauce for guests to add to the baguettes as desired.

Advance preparation: Fill the baguettes 2 hours before, cover, and chill. Heat as above. *Freezing: Freeze the garlic butter 4 weeks before.*

Italian BLT focaccia

This Italian sandwich with hot pancetta is a twist on the classic BLT. MAKES 10

10 yellow or red tomatoes, halved lengthwise
1 cup olive oil
A large pinch of sugar
20 slices pancetta or thinly cut bacon
Ten 4-inch squares herbed focaccia, split
2 cups (1 lb) ricotta cheese
1 cup purple or green basil leaves
Salt & freshly ground pepper to taste

Preheat the oven to 375°F. Put the tomatoes skin-side down in a roasting pan, drizzle with ¼ cup of the olive oil, and sprinkle with the sugar plus some salt and pepper.
Roast the tomatoes for 30 minutes or until soft and slightly charred. Remove from the pan while warm, transfer to paper towels and let cool.
Fry the pancetta or bacon for 2–3 minutes or until very crisp. Drain and cool on paper towels.
Drizzle the cut surfaces of the focaccia with the remaining olive oil. Cover with the pancetta or bacon.
Spread on the ricotta. Add the tomatoes, then the basil. Put the lids on and serve.

Advance preparation: Roast, cool, and chill the tomatoes up to 2 days before. Fry the pancetta or bacon 1 day before, cover, and chill. Make the sandwiches 2 hours ahead, cover, and chill. *Freezing: The pancetta can be cooked and frozen up to 4 weeks ahead. Crisp in a preheated 375°F oven for 3–4 minutes. Cool before serving.*

left Italian BLT focaccia

Bagels with red pepper & olive relish

Bagels with red pepper & olive relish

Bagels with smoked salmon and cream cheese are a winner, but they are also good spread with mascarpone and this relish. MAKES 10

3 red bell peppers
5 bagels, split
1 cup pitted black olives, coarsely chopped
¼ cup capers in balsamic vinegar, drained
⅓ cup coarsely chopped fresh flat-leaf parsley
2 tblsp olive oil
1 cup (8 oz) mascarpone cheese
Salt & freshly ground pepper to taste

Broil the peppers until the skins are blackened. Place in a bowl, cover with plastic wrap, and let stand for 10 minutes.
Peel and seed the peppers. Set the flesh aside to cool, then chop it coarsely.
Toast both sides of the bagels lightly and let cool.
Mix the chopped peppers with the olives, capers, parsley, and olive oil, then season.
Spread the mascarpone on the cut side of the bagels, spoon on the red pepper and olive relish, and serve.

Advance preparation: Make the relish 3 days ahead without the parsley; cover and chill. Add the parsley and top the bagels 1 hour before.
Freezing: Not suitable.

Soft-shell crab sandwich & zucchini fries

Crabs and shoestring fries crammed between slices of black rye bread are sheer bliss! The fries and crab can be served individually, but you will need lots of napkins. MAKES 10

4 oz water crackers
20 slices black rye bread
Vegetable oil for frying
Salt & freshly ground pepper to taste

for the tartare sauce
Heaping ⅓ cup mayonnaise
2 heaping tblsp coarsely chopped
   dill pickles or gherkins
1 heaping tblsp coarsely chopped fresh parsley
1 small red onion, finely chopped
1 heaping tblsp finely snipped fresh chives
2 heaping tsp capers, drained
for the zucchini fries
1lb zucchini
3 tblsp all-purpose flour
for the soft-shell crabs
3 tblsp all-purpose flour
Ten 4-oz soft-shell crabs
2 medium eggs, lightly beaten
A few drops of Tabasco sauce

Mix all the ingredients together for the tartare sauce and season.
Pulse the crackers in a blender or processor 7–8 times to make coarse crumbs.
Spread the tartare sauce over 10 slices of the rye bread.
Cut the zucchini into ⅓-inch-thick sticks, ideally using a mandoline. Toss them in flour with lots of seasoning.
Season the flour for the crabs and then toss them in this mixture to coat well.
Mix the eggs and Tabasco together, dip the crabs in to coat, and then roll them in the cracker crumbs.
Heat a large pan of oil for deep-frying to 300°F and preheat the oven to 350°F. Deep-fry the crabs in batches in the hot oil for 3 minutes or until crisp and golden brown. Drain on paper towels and keep warm in the oven.
Deep-fry the zucchini in batches in the oil for 1 minute or until crisp and golden, stirring constantly. Drain them on paper towels and sprinkle with salt. Keep warm.
Put a soft-shell crab on top of each piece of sauced bread, add the some zucchini fries, and top with the remaining slices of bread. Serve immediately.

Advance preparation: Make the tartare sauce and the cracker crumbs up to 2 days before. Cover and chill the sauce and store the crumbs in an airtight container. Cut the fries up to 4 hours ahead, cover, and chill. Fry to order.
Freezing: Not suitable.

Muffuletta

Muffuletta is native to New Orleans. It is a macho, chunky sandwich, great for picnics, or for when you know that your guests will have demanding and hearty appetites. You can also fill individual rolls, such as ciabatta, with these layers of salami, cheese, and olive salad. SERVES 10

2 cups pitted black olives, coarsely chopped
2 large roasted red bell peppers (see col. 1, opposite), peeled, seeded & coarsely chopped; or 1½ cups (10 oz) canned red pimientos, drained, rinsed & coarsely chopped
1 large clove garlic, crushed
⅔ cup olive oil
1 tblsp fresh lemon juice
Two 14-oz rustic round bread loaves, flavored with olives, tomato, or cheese
5 oz sliced salami
3 cups curly endive
12 oz taleggio or mozzarella cheese, sliced
5 oz sliced mortadella
2 cups arugula leaves
Freshly ground pepper to taste

Combine the olives, peppers, garlic, olive oil, lemon juice, and black pepper.

Cut the breads across the middle and remove the crumb from both the top and bottom halves. (Reserve and freeze the crumb for another recipe.)

Divide half the olive mixture between the bottom of each loaf and, in the following order, arrange the salami, curly endive, taleggio or mozzarella, the rest of the olive mixture, mortadella, and arugula, in layers inside them.

Replace the bread lids, cover with plastic wrap, and chill for at least 1 hour before serving. Cut each of the muffulettas into 5 wedges and serve.

Advance preparation: Make the olive mixture 3 days ahead but do not add the lemon juice until assembling; cover and chill. Fill the bread up to 6 hours before, cover, and chill.
Freezing: Not suitable.

right Soft-shell crab sandwich & zucchini fries

Thanksgiving roll with sweet potato fries

Thanksgiving usually means roast turkey, sweet potatoes, cornbread stuffing, and cranberry sauce. Here I am celebrating Thanksgiving, not traditionally, but instead served in a roll. There is turkey and grilled corn relish inside and some chunky sweet potato fries served as a side order. I have never been a fan of cranberry sauce, but if it is an essential part of Thanksgiving for you, go ahead and add some. MAKES 10

2 lb sliced roasted turkey

10 soft brown rolls, halved

Heaping ⅓ cup mayonnaise

A few leaves of curly endive

Grilled Corn and Red Pepper Relish (page 63)

3 heaping tblsp cranberry sauce (optional)

for the sweet potato fries

2½ lb unpeeled sweet potatoes cut into chunky fries

Vegetable oil for deep-frying

Salt to taste

Preheat the oven to 375°F. Spread the turkey slices out on an ovenproof dish and heat them in the oven for 12–15 minutes or until piping hot.

Wash and dry the sweet potatoes very well. Heat the oil in a deep-fat fryer to 300°F. Fry the sweet potatoes in batches for 4 minutes. Drain on paper towels and then fry again in batches for 1 minute or until crisp and golden. Drain on paper towels and lightly salt. Keep warm.

Spread the rolls with mayonnaise, divide

Thanksgiving roll with sweet potato fries

the endive among them, put the turkey on top, and finish with some relish or cranberry sauce. Replace the tops of the rolls and serve them with the hot fries.

Advance preparation: Make the corn relish up to 1 day before, cover, and chill. Cut the fries up to 2 hours before and fry them for 4 minutes up to 1 hour ahead. Drain. Refry for 1 minute to order. *Freezing: Not suitable.*

Sloppy Joe pita breads

Here the American favorite, sloppy Joes, is given a Tex-Mex feel. Typically served in toasted burger buns, I have swapped them for pita breads as the pockets make natural containers for the spicy beef. You will have to fill the sloppy Joes to order, otherwise the bread gets too soft. Wrap them in a napkin or some waxed paper, as they make a real mess and will spill all over the place. They are great, filling party food but not dainty eating! MAKES 10

Ten 4-inch pita breads
for the beef mixture
1 onion, chopped
1½ tblsp finely chopped jalapeno chili
1 large clove garlic, crushed
¼ cup vegetable oil
1½ lb ground beef
1 tblsp ground cumin
14 oz canned chopped tomatoes
⅔ cup tomato ketchup
Salt & freshly ground pepper to taste
for the topping
2 recipes Avocado Relish (page 63)
1 hot red chili, finely diced
⅔ cup sour cream

Sauté the onion, chili, and garlic together in oil in a large frying pan over medium heat for about 7–8 minutes or until soft and translucent.

Add the beef and cook over high heat for 4–5 minutes, stirring all the time, or until lightly browned. Drain off and discard all the fat. Add the cumin and seasoning and cook for 1 minute.

Reduce the heat to medium and add the canned tomatoes and ketchup. Season and cook for 20–30 minutes or until the mixture is thick but still sloppy.

Add the diced chili to the avocado relish. Cut the tops off the pita breads.

Spoon the beef mixture into the pita breads. Top with a dollop of sour cream and the avocado relish. Wrap in a napkin and serve immediately.

Advance preparation: Make the beef mixture 2 days before, cool, cover, and chill. Reheat in a pan for 15–20 minutes or until piping hot. Make the avocado relish up to 1 hour before and cover. *Freezing: The beef mixture can be frozen up to 4 weeks ahead. Reheat as above.*

Right: *Give those old-fashioned food favorites a twist — these lip-smacking spicy wedges are made from potatoes and served with a tamarind-flavored ketchup for dipping.* **Below:** *when there is no room in the fridge, keep beers and other bottled drinks cold by piling them in buckets filled with ice. Your local wine merchant is the best source of bulk ice — they usually rent glasses for parties, too.*

Left: *Garlic bread is perennially popular. Here it is piled high with juicy warm shrimp for a hearty hand-held snack.* **Right:** *It is not necessary to continually walk round the party offering finger foods to guests. Spread platters of food out on a simply decorated table that you have moved to one side of the room and let guests serve themselves. Make sure there is plenty of space around the table.*

housewarming

Above: *Elegance is not always desired, especially at informal events, so for a housewarming make some finger food that is hot and hearty. Pile beef chili into pita bread pockets, then top with sour cream, garnish with avocado relish, and wrap in a colorful napkin for a filling snack.*

Left: *A new take on crudités. Crisp vegetables and shellfish are matched with a creamy bean dip.*

Left: *The clever party host will make use of good things from favorite delis and restaurants. Here, bottled chutneys and pickles are served with poppadums from an Indian restaurant.* Above: *Muffuletta, a loaf of bread filled with Italian deli items, is easy to make, filling, and tasty.* Right: *Chicken wings are easy to nibble on when held with the fingers. Give them a spicy treatment with red curry paste.*

Bay scallops with Thai dipping sauce

I love this simple fishy canapé with its pert flavors of cilantro and pickled ginger. The dipping sauce is also excellent as a dressing for chicken or fish salads. MAKES 20

for the Thai dipping sauce
2 tblsp Thai fish sauce
1 tblsp fresh lime juice
2 tblsp palm sugar or dark brown sugar
1 red bird's-eye chili, finely sliced
1 scallion, finely sliced
2 tsp finely sliced red onion
2 tsp finely chopped cucumber
2 tsp finely chopped carrot
2 tsp chopped peanuts
for the scallops
20 bay scallops
20 fresh cilantro leaves
20 pieces pickled ginger
Sesame oil for greasing
You will also need 20 toothpicks

Make the dipping sauce by combining all the ingredients and stirring until the sugar has dissolved. Pour into a small bowl.
Heat a ridged cast-iron grill pan and grease it lightly with the sesame oil. Sear the scallops on both sides for a total of 2–3 minutes. Transfer to some paper towels to cool. Alternatively, light a charcoal fire and cook the scallops on an oiled rack set 4–6 inches above medium-hot coals for 2–3 minutes on each side, then let cool on paper towels.
Skewer the scallops on the toothpicks with the cilantro leaves and pickled ginger and serve with the dipping sauce.

Advance preparation: Make the dipping sauce up to 2 days ahead, cover, and chill. Cook the scallops up to 4 hours before, cover, and chill. Assemble 1 hour before serving, cover, and chill.
Freezing: Not suitable.

Italian vegetable skewers

Mix and match the vegetables on these skewers — they do not have to be identical. If you like, offer them with a pesto dip, or brush with pesto before serving. MAKES 10

6 bocconcini (tiny mozzarella)
6 sun-dried tomato halves in oil, drained
6 yellow or red plum cherry tomatoes
3 yellow or green pattypan squash, halved
½ small red or yellow bell pepper, seeded and cut into eighths
3 baby zucchini, cut into 2-inch pieces
3 scallions, cut into 2-inch pieces
1 small red onion, cut into 6 wedges through the root
¼ cup olive oil + extra for greasing
2 cloves garlic, crushed

Italian vegetable skewers

Salt & freshly ground pepper to taste
You will also need 10 bamboo skewers

Soak the skewers in a bowl of water for
2 hours. This will keep them from burning.
Marinate all the ingredients in the oil,
garlic, and seasoning for 30 minutes.
Thread a mixture of the bocconcini and
5 different vegetables onto each skewer.

Cook on a hot ridged cast-iron grill pan or
under the broiler for 5–7 minutes, turning
once or twice, until the vegetables are
crisp-tender. Alternatively, place the
skewers on an oiled rack set 4–6 inches
above medium-hot charcoal. Turn them
after 5 minutes or so and cook for 5
minutes longer or until done. Serve the
skewers hot or cold.

Advance preparation: Marinate the
cheese and vegetables up to 12 hours
ahead, cover, and chill. If serving the
skewers cold, cook them up to 6 hours
in advance, cover, and chill.
Freezing: Not suitable.

Sticky red curry chicken wings

*Sticky and shiny fire-engine red, these
Thai-flavored chicken wings can be
barbecued or roasted.* MAKES 10

½ cup palm sugar or dark brown sugar
½ cup tomato paste
¼ cup Thai red curry paste
2 tsp salt
10 chicken wings
Vegetable oil for greasing

Heat the palm sugar and tomato paste in
a pan over low heat for 4–5 minutes or
until the sugar has dissolved.
Remove from the heat, stir in the curry
paste and salt, and let cool.
Pour the cooled mixture over the chicken
wings and toss well to coat. Cover and
marinate in the fridge for at least 4 hours.
Preheat the oven to 375°F. Transfer the
chicken wings to a lightly oiled roasting
pan and spread them out.
Roast the wings for 35–40 minutes or
until cooked and slightly charred.
Alternatively, place the wings on an oiled
rack 4–6 inches above medium-hot
charcoal and cook for 12–15 minutes,
turning once. Serve hot or cold.

Advance preparation: Cook, cover, and
chill up to 1 day ahead. If serving the
wings hot, reheat at 375°F for 20
minutes or until piping hot.
*Freezing: Freeze the cooked chicken
wings up to 4 weeks ahead. Reheat as
above, or defrost and serve cold.*

Passion fruit & papaya wontons

Wonton wrappers need not be restricted to savory foods; they are just as good with sweet toppings like tropical fruits. Dusted with icing sugar and cinnamon, they are also an easy accompaniment for desserts such as kissel (page 132) or granita. MAKES 10

Vegetable oil for deep-frying
10 wonton wrappers
1 heaping tblsp cream cheese
¼ small papaya, thinly sliced
Seeds from 2 passion fruit
Confectioners' sugar, for dusting

Heat the oil in a pan to 350°F and fry the wonton wrappers for about 30 seconds or until golden brown. Drain well on paper towels and let cool.

Top each fried wonton wrapper with a little of the cream cheese, a few slices of papaya, and some passion fruit seeds.

Dust the wontons with icing sugar and serve immediately.

Advance preparation: Fry the wrappers up to 12 hours in advance and store in an airtight container. Prepare the fruits 3–4 hours before serving, cover, and chill. *Freezing: Not suitable.*

Elderflower jellies

Bottled elderflower cordial makes beautifully scented, pop-in-the-mouth jellies that I have studded with fresh berries. MAKES 20

6 leaves gelatin
¾ cup + 1 tblsp boiling water
⅔ cup elderflower cordial or
   raspberry liqueur
10 raspberries
20 blueberries
You will also need 2 trays of 10 ice cubes

Soak the gelatin in some cold water for 10 minutes, then squeeze it to remove the excess water.

Put the boiling water into a pitcher, add the gelatin, and stir until dissolved. Pour in the cordial or liqueur, stir, and let cool for 10 minutes.

Divide the raspberries among one of the ice-cube trays and the blueberries among the other. Pour the elderflower mixture over these fruits and then chill for 5 hours or until set.

Dip the ice-cube trays in very hot water, just up to the level of the jelly, count to 5, and remove from the water.

Use a small sharp knife to loosen the edges of the jellies and turn out onto a plate lined with plastic wrap. Transfer the jellies to a serving dish using a metal spatula.

Advance preparation: Make the jellies up to 2 days ahead, cover, and chill. *Freezing: Not suitable.*

Fruited bruschetta

You can use all different types of breads and toppings for sweet bruschetta. Try chocolate bread with coffee ice cream drizzled with chocolate sauce or maple syrup. A spoonful of Red Berry Kissel (page 132) with a dollop of Lemon Syllabub (page 81) is also a glorious combination. MAKES 20

Fruited bruschetta

10 slices brioche, cut from individual
  brioches
½ cup mascarpone
1 peach, thinly sliced
10 strawberries, thinly sliced
¾ cup raspberries
for the mango & passion fruit bruschetta
10 slices fruit bread
⅔ cup heavy cream, lightly whipped
3 passion fruit, seeded and juiced
1 small mango, thinly sliced
A small piece of fresh coconut, unskinned

Toast the slices of brioche and fruited
bread lightly on either side under a
preheated broiler or in a hot ridged
cast-iron grill pan. Let cool.

Spoon the mascarpone onto the brioche
and arrange the peaches, strawberries,
and raspberries on top.

Mix the whipped cream with the seeds
and juice of 1 passion fruit and spoon it
onto the fruit bread. Top the cream with
the mango and the seeds and juice of the
remaining passion fruit.

Make fine shavings of coconut using a
vegetable peeler and arrange them on top
of the fruit before serving.

Advance preparation: Toast the breads
and keep covered. Add the passionfruit
to the cream, slice the peaches and
strawberries, and chill 1–2 hours ahead.
Top the bruschetta 30 minutes before.
Freezing: Not suitable.

Summer berry tartlets

Yogurt cheese topped with tropical fruit makes a good alternative to the mascarpone and red berries in these tartlets. The fail-safe pastry recipe given here can be used for a number of sweet dishes. It is not worth making smaller amounts of the dough, so divide it into batches and freeze for use as required. This recipe will yield 2 lb of sweet pastry, which in turn will make: 120 mini (1½-inch) tartlets; twenty 4-inch shallow tarts; or three 10-inch shallow tarts. To make savory pastry, simply omit the sugar. MAKES 12

for the sweet pastry (makes 2 lb)
3 cups all-purpose flour, sifted +
  extra for dusting
1¼ cups confectioners' sugar, sifted

A pinch of salt
1 cup (2 sticks) unsalted butter, diced
1 egg, beaten
1 tblsp cold water
for the filling
½ cup mascarpone cheese
2 cups fresh berries, such as blackberries,
  halved strawberries, raspberries, and
  red or black currants
A few sprigs of mint to decorate, if
  using strawberries
Confectioners' sugar, for dusting
You will also need a set of twelve 1½-inch tartlet pans and a 2-inch round cutter

Put the flour, icing sugar, salt, and butter together in a food processor and pulse 7–8 times until the mixture resembles fine bread crumbs. Turn into a bowl, add the egg and water, and stir to blend.

Knead well to make a firm dough. Wrap about one eighth of the pastry in plastic wrap and chill for 30 minutes before using; freeze the remainder in batches for use in other recipes.

Roll the chilled pastry out thinly on a lightly floured surface and use the cutter to cut out 12 circles. Carefully line the tartlet pans, pressing the pastry down into the bottom and up the sides of the pans. Trim away any excess, lightly prick the shells with a fork, and chill for 30 minutes.

Preheat the oven to 375°F and bake the tartlets for 10 minutes or until golden. Cool for 10 minutes before transferring from the pans to a plate.

Fill the tartlet shells with the mascarpone, divide the fruits among them, decorating any strawberries with mint leaves, and lightly dust with confectioners' sugar.

Advance preparation: Make the pastry 2 days ahead, cover with plastic wrap, and chill. Allow to soften for 20 minutes before using. Bake the tartlet shells 1 day ahead and store in an airtight container. Fill 45 minutes before serving.
Freezing: Freeze the pastry in batches 4 weeks ahead. The baked tartlet cases can be frozen 3 weeks ahead and crisped in a preheated 350°F oven for 2–3 minutes. Cool before assembling.

French apple tartlets

These are miniature versions of the classic French apple tart. MAKES 12

⅛ recipe (4 oz) Sweet Pastry (left)
Flour for dusting
2 small Granny Smith apples,
  peeled & cored
1 tblsp confectioners' sugar
You will also need 12 square tartlet pans or a set of 12 round tartlet pans 1½ inches in diameter and a 2-inch square or round cutter

Roll the pastry out thinly on a lightly floured surface. Cut out 12 squares or circles and use them to line the tartlet pans. Trim away any excess, prick the

French apple tartlets

shells with a fork, and chill for 30 minutes.

Preheat the oven to 375°F. Cut the apples into 6 wedges, then cut 72 very thin slices from the apples and coarsely chop the rest.

Fill the tartlets with the chopped apples and arrange the slices on top. Place on a baking sheet and bake for 15 minutes or until the fruit is cooked and the pastry golden.

Dust the top of the tartlets with confectioners' sugar and quickly heat under a preheated broiler to glaze the apple slices.

Cool for 10 minutes, then transfer from the pans to a plate. Serve warm or cold.

Advance preparation: One day before, line the tartlet pans with pastry, cover and chill.

Freezing: The tartlet shells can be frozen unbaked in their tins for 1 week, then filled and baked straight from the freezer.

Lemon syllabub puffs

Choux pastry is highly versatile, as it can be used for both sweet and savory foods. As well as this syllabub, mascarpone and red berries, Saffron Cream (page 137), Chunky Pesto (page 43), or lemony crab (page 33) are good fillings to use. MAKES 16

for the choux pastry
⅓ cup water
2 tblsp unsalted butter +
  extra for greasing
3 tblsp all-purpose flour, sifted
A pinch of salt
1 small egg, lightly beaten
for the lemon syllabub
2 tsp fresh lemon juice
2 tsp sherry or brandy
1 tblsp sweet white wine
1 tsp sugar
¼ cup heavy cream
16 crystallized violets to decorate
Confectioners' sugar, for dusting
You will also need a pastry bag and a plain ½-inch pastry tip

Make the choux by gently melting the butter in a saucepan with the water. Then, bring the water to a boil, remove from the heat, and add the flour and salt.

Return the pan to low heat and stir the dough vigorously with a wooden spoon for 3–4 minutes or until the mixture cleanly leaves the sides of the pan. Cool slightly.

Add the egg to the dough and beat until you have a smooth, glossy mixture.

Preheat the oven to 400°F. Place small spoonfuls of the pastry well apart on a lightly greased baking sheet. Bake for 10–12 minutes or until crisp.

Make a small slit in the top of each puff, return to the oven, and leave the door ajar for 5 minutes to dry them out.

Cool on a rack and then cut a small wedge from the tops of the puffs.

Lemon syllabub puffs

Mix the lemon juice, sherry, and wine together. Add the sugar and stir to dissolve. Slowly pour this mixture onto the cream, beating with a whisk until it forms soft peaks.

Spoon the syllabub into a pastry bag fitted with a pastry tip and pipe it into the puffs. Decorate with the violets, lightly dust with confectioners' sugar, and serve.

Advance preparation: Make the syllabub and puffs 1 day in advance. Cover and chill the syllabub and whisk briefly if it separates. Put the pastries in an airtight container; crisp for 2–3 minutes at 350°F, then cool. Fill the puffs up to 1 hour before serving.
Freezing: Freeze the baked puffs 3 weeks ahead, crisp, and fill as above.

Yogurt ices

Desserts do not always have to be grown-up, and these frozen yogurt cones are a fun way to end a casual meal. MAKES 20

20 ice cream cones
for the lemon curd ices
2 cups (1 lb) plain yogurt
1 cup (8 oz) lemon curd or other
   fruit curd
⅓ cup candied citrus peel, finely sliced
for the strawberry ices
2 cups (1 lb) plain yogurt
½ cup sugar
⅔ cup strawberries, hulled & quartered
   + 10 whole strawberries
You will also need an ice cream scoop

Whisk the first batch of yogurt and the lemon curd together in a plastic bowl for 2 minutes or until light and aerated.
Scrape down the sides of the bowl and freeze for 1 hour. Break up the semi-frozen mixture with a fork, then whisk again for 2 minutes. Scrape down the sides again and freeze for 1 hour more. Repeat once more, transfer to a lidded container, and freeze for at least 4 hours.
Repeat the same procedure for the strawberry ices, whisking only the yogurt and sugar together. After the third whisking, add the strawberries, whisk again for 10 seconds, transfer to a lidded container, and freeze for at least 4 hours.
Remove the frozen ices from the freezer, allow to soften slightly, and make into balls with an ice cream scoop.
Top 10 of the cones with a scoop of the lemon ice and sprinkle with the citrus peel. Fill the remaining cones with the strawberry ice, then decorate with the strawberries and serve immediately.

Advance preparation: Slice the citrus peel up to 1 week ahead and store in an airtight container.
Freezing: Make the ices up to 3 weeks ahead and remove from the freezer about 20 minutes before serving.

left Yogurt ices

Ice cream–filled brioche

Chocolate cups with ice cream

You can buy both the chocolate cups and the ice cream for an instant, bite-sized indulgence. MAKES 10

A selection of ice cream or sorbet, such
   as chocolate, coffee, orange, or vanilla
10 mini chocolate cups
You will also need a melon baller

Make small balls of ice cream with the melon baller and arrange one in each of the chocolate cups. Serve.

Advance preparation: See below.
Freezing: Freeze the filled cups 2 days ahead in an airtight container. Serve straight from the freezer.

Ice cream–filled brioches

This is another effortless recipe that makes good use of store-bought items. MAKES 10

10 bite-sized brioches, muffins, or cakes
Heaping ½ cup ice cream, such as
   pistachio or strawberry
Confectioners' sugar for dusting

Cut the tops off the brioches, hollow them out, and then spoon in the ice cream.
Replace the lids, lightly dust with confectioners' sugar, and serve immediately.

Advance preparation: Hollow out the brioches 4 hours before and cover.
Freezing: Fill 3–4 days in advance and freeze. Let the brioches soften for a few minutes before dusting with confectioners' sugar.

Heart-shaped chocolate cookies

Heart-shaped chocolate cookies

Make these heart-shaped cookies when you are feeling particularly romantic, or to serve at weddings — perhaps giving every guest one as they leave. I find the chocolate cookie dough recipe very useful: This quantity of pastry will also yield approximately 120 1½-inch cookies or 2-inch numerals for decorating birthday cakes or for serving as cookies; or sixty-five 2½-inch cookies for afternoon tea or to accompany desserts. MAKES 12

for the chocolate cookie dough (makes 1¾ lb)
¾ cup (1½ sticks) unsalted butter, softened
1⅓ cups granulated sugar
1 egg, beaten
1⅓ cups all-purpose flour + extra for rolling
1¼ cups unsweetened cocoa powder
A pinch of salt

for the icing
1 egg white, lightly beaten
1¼ cups confectioners' sugar, sifted
You will also need 3 heart-shaped cutters approximately 2 inches, 3 inches, and 4 inches wide; a pastry bag, a ⅛-inch plain pastry tip; and twelve 12-inch lengths of ribbon

Beat the butter and sugar for the chocolate cookie dough together until light and creamy. Add the egg and beat well for another 1–2 minutes.

Sift in the flour, cocoa, and salt and knead to combine. Wrap the dough in plastic wrap and chill for 1 hour.

Roll the dough out to a thickness of ¼ inch on a lightly floured surface. Cut out 12 hearts using the 4-inch cutter and transfer to baking sheets.

Use the 3-inch cutter to cut out a heart from the center of each large heart. Transfer these smaller hearts to another baking sheet and trim, using the 2-inch cutter, so they fit inside the large hearts.

Make a hole large enough to take some thin ribbon in the top of each cookie, using a skewer or a small sharp knife. Chill for 30 minutes.

Preheat the oven to 350°F and bake the hearts for 8 minutes or until slightly darker in color. Transfer them to a wire rack to cool.

Beat together the egg white and confectioners' sugar to make the icing. Spoon into a pastry bag and decorate the cookies as desired with hearts and lettering.

Tie a large and a small cookie together with some ribbon and serve.

Advance preparation: Make the dough up to 2 days before, cover with plastic wrap, and chill. Let the dough soften for 20 minutes before using. Bake and decorate the cookies 2 days before and store in single layers in airtight containers. *Freezing: Freeze the dough in batches 4 weeks ahead. The baked cookies can be made and frozen 3 weeks before. Crisp in a preheated 350°F oven for 3–4 minutes. Cool and decorate up to 2 days ahead. Store as above.*

Chocolate cookies with coffee-praline cream

These chocolate and coffee cream cookies, together with the ice cream–filled chocolate cups (page 83), make a perfectly delicious ending to a cocktail party. MAKES 10

⅛ recipe Chocolate Cookie Dough (see left)
Flour for rolling
3 oz semisweet chocolate, chopped
for the praline
1 heaping tblsp almonds or hazelnuts with skins
1 heaping tblsp sugar
for the coffee cream
¼ cup heavy cream
1 tsp strong cold sweetened coffee or Kahlúa
You will also need a 1¾-inch fluted cutter, a pastry bag and a ½-inch star pastry tip

Roll the dough out to a thickness of ⅛ inch on a lightly floured surface. Cut out 10 cookies and transfer to a baking sheet. Chill for 30 minutes.

Preheat the oven to 350°F and bake the cookies for 8 minutes or until slightly darker in color. Transfer them to a wire rack to cool.

Heat the nuts and sugar in a small pan over low heat without stirring, until the sugar has melted to a deep golden color. This will take about 8–10 minutes. Pour onto a lightly greased baking sheet to cool.

Break the set praline into pieces and quickly pulse in a blender 7–8 times or until you have fine crumbs. Alternatively, put the praline in a heavy plastic bag and crush it with a rolling pin.

Melt the chocolate in a bowl over a pan of simmering water, pour it onto a plastic tray, and set aside to cool. When it has set, draw a cheese slicer across the surface to make curls and then chill them.

Beat the cream until it justs holds its shape. Stir in the cold coffee or liqueur, then fold in the praline.

Spoon the flavored cream into a pastry bag, pipe onto the biscuits, and decorate with chocolate curls. Serve.

Advance preparation: Make the cookies, praline, and chocolate curls 4 days before. Store the cookies and praline in airtight containers and the chocolate curls in the fridge. Assemble 30 minutes before.

Freezing: Freeze the baked cookies up to 3 weeks before. Crisp them in a preheated 350°F oven for 3–4 minutes. Cool.

Happy birthday cupcakes

I think these bite-sized orange cupcakes are a fun way to celebrate a birthday, anniversary, or festive occasion. Pipe a message on them and decorate as your artistic talents allow. MAKES 48

for the orange cupcakes
7 tblsp unsalted butter, softened
  + extra for greasing
½ cup granulated sugar
Finely grated zest of 1½ oranges
1 medium egg
2 tblsp orange juice
1 cup self-rising flour, sifted
for the glacé icing
2 cups confectioners' sugar, sifted
¼ cup warm water
1 tblsp orange flower water or
  strained orange juice
for the royal icing
3 large egg whites, lightly beaten
3½ cups confectioners' sugar, sifted
2 different food colorings
You will also need four 12-cup mini muffin pans, 48 small paper liners, 2 pastry bags, 2 small star pastry tips, and 1 small plain pastry tip

Preheat the oven to 350°F and line the muffin cups with the paper liners.
Beat the butter, sugar, and orange zest together for 2 minutes or until light and creamy. Beat in the egg and orange juice, then fold in the flour.
Divide this mixture among the muffin cups and bake 20–25 minutes or until risen and golden. Transfer from the pans to a wire rack to cool.
Make the glacé icing by putting the sugar in a bowl and making a well in the center.

Happy birthday cupcakes

Slowly incorporate the water until the icing is very smooth. Mix in the orange flower water or strained orange juice.
Use the glacé icing immediately or a skin will form on it. Spoon the icing onto the cakes and let set for about 1 hour.
Mix the egg whites and sugar together for the royal icing until stiff but pipeable. Divide into thirds and tint one batch with one color and another batch with another color, and leave the remainder white.
Decorate the edges of the cakes with the white royal icing using a star tip. Pipe the

message on the cakes with one color, using the other star tip. Use the other colored icing and the plain tip to decorate the rest with hearts and flowers. Let dry for 2 hours before serving.

Advance preparation: Decorate the cakes 2 days ahead and store in single layers in airtight containers.
Freezing: Freeze the undecorated cakes 1 week before. Decorate as above.

Vanilla shortbreads with crème fraîche & lime curd

These oh-so-pretty scallop-edged shortbreads are good enough to serve on their own, but the easy crème fraîche and lime curd topping is a nice touch, particularly for celebratory occasions. MAKES 12

for the vanilla shortbreads

4 tblsp unsalted butter + extra
  for greasing
¾ cup all-purpose flour, sifted
  + extra for rolling
2 tblsp vanilla sugar
A pinch of salt

for the crème fraîche & lime curd topping

2 tblsp crème fraîche, or lightly
  whipped cream
2 tsp lime or lemon curd
A few shavings of candied citrus
  peel to decorate

You will also need a 2½-inch fluted cutter and a ¼-inch plain pastry tip

Process the butter, flour and salt together in a food processor until it resembles fine bread crumbs. Mix in the sugar. Turn out onto a lightly floured surface and lightly knead to make a firm dough.

Roll the dough out to a thickness of ¼ inch, cut out 12 rounds, and place them on a lightly greased baking sheet.

Use the pastry tip to cut out a ring of small circles around the inside edges of the shortbread rounds to decorate them. Chill for 30 minutes.

Preheat the oven to 350°F and bake the shortbreads for 12 minutes or until they are light golden. Transfer them to a wire rack to cool.

Spoon the crème fraîche or cream onto the shortbreads and top with a little lime curd. Swirl the two together with a skewer, then decorate with the peel and serve.

Advance preparation: Make and bake the shortbreads up to 4 days before and store in an airtight container. Top them 30 minutes before serving.
Freezing: Freeze the baked shortbreads up to 3 weeks before and crisp in a preheated 350°F oven for 3–4 minutes. Cool before topping.

Scones with cream & jams

Speed from start to finish is essential when making scones to achieve a light texture. If clotted cream and jam are just too rich for your taste, yogurt cheese and honey is a more virtuous substitute. MAKES 10

for the scones

¾ cup self-rising flour, sifted
  + extra for rolling
2 tblsp unsalted butter, diced
  + extra for greasing
A pinch of salt
1 tblsp sugar
¼ cup milk mixed with 1 tblsp fresh
  lemon juice to sour
1 tblsp milk for glazing

for the filling

2 tblsp clotted cream or whipped cream
2 tblsp jam, such as apricot, black
  currant or raspberry

You will also need a 1½-inch plain round cutter

Rub the flour, butter and salt together until the mixture resembles fine crumbs. Mix in the sugar, then quickly stir in the milk, which has been soured with the lemon juice, to make a soft dough.

Turn the dough out onto a floured surface and knead it very lightly.

Roll the dough out gently to a thickness of ½ inch and cut out the scones. Reroll any trimmings and cut out, remembering they will not be as light as the first batch, nor will they rise as evenly.

Place on a greased baking sheet and brush the tops with milk. Let rest for 5 minutes.

Preheat the oven to 425°F and bake the scones for 7 minutes or until well risen and golden brown. Transfer to a wire rack to cool slightly.

Split the scones, spoon in the cream and jam, and serve.

Advance preparation: Bake the scones up to 8 hours before and store in an airtight container. Fill 1 hour before serving, cover, and keep cool.
Freezing: Freeze the baked scones 3 weeks ahead and warm in a preheated 350°F oven for 2–3 minutes. Cool, then fill as above.

Tiny Christmas puddings on cinnamon shortbreads

Dramatic in spite of their diminutive size, these Christmas puddings are always greeted with childish delight. Serve these and the Christmas dinner tartlets together at a festive cocktail party. MAKES 10

½ recipe Vanilla Shortbread (left) made
  with ½ tsp ground cinnamon
Butter for greasing
Flour for dusting
One 4-oz Christmas or plum pudding
2 tblsp ready-made white marzipan
2 tblsp ready-made white icing
Red & green food coloring
Confectioners' sugar for dusting
1 tsp apricot jam

You will also need a 1-inch and a 1½-inch fluted round cutter, and a tiny holly leaf cutter

Follow the basic vanilla shortbread recipe as given opposite, adding the ground cinnamon to the sifted flour.

Preheat the oven to 350°F. Roll the dough out to a thickness of ¼ inch on a lightly floured surface, then cut out 10 rounds and place them on a lightly greased baking sheet.

Bake the shortbreads in the oven for 12 minutes or until light golden. Transfer them to a wire rack to cool.

Divide the Christmas or plum pudding into 10 pieces and roll each into a ball.

Break off a third of the marzipan and add a few drops of red coloring to it.

Add green coloring to the remaining marzipan and knead both batches well to incorporate the colors.

Roll out the green marzipan on a surface lightly dusted with confectioners' sugar and cut out 20 holly leaves using the holly cutter.

Make 30 tiny berries from the red marzipan.

Roll the white icing out on a surface lightly dusted with confectioners' sugar and, using the 1-inch fluted cutter, cut out 10 small circles of icing.

Cover the top of each Christmas pudding ball with a small fluted circle of icing.

Moisten a fine pastry brush, dampen the icing leaves and berries, and stick them on top of the fluted circles.

Turn the oven to 375°F. Place the decorated puddings onto the cinnamon shortbreads and transfer them to a baking sheet. Cover loosely with foil.

Heat the puddings though in the oven for 12–15 minutes or until hot. Serve.

Advance preparation: Bake the cinnamon shortbreads and roll and decorate the Christmas puddings up to 4 days before. Store separately in airtight containers.

Freezing: Freeze the baked shortbreads up to 3 weeks ahead and crisp in a preheated 350°F oven for 2–3 minutes. Cool before use.

Tiny Christmas puddings on cinnamon shortbreads

cocktails

Clockwise from top right:

A friendly bowl of mixed nuts glazed with sesame seeds; tropical fruit and soft cheese top a crisply fried wonton wrapper; lay out the brioches, crème fraîche, and caviar and let guests help themselves; buy a jar of pickled veggies and pile onto rice crackers for a no-effort canapé with class; chives tie crispy duck pancakes into a roll for easy, elegant eating.

Above left: *A classic combination of vodka, glistening salmon roe, sour cream, and blini. Make it even more special by adding edible gold leaf to the drink.* Above right: *We've come a long way from diced cheese and cocktail onions on toothpicks. Here, seared scallops, fresh herbs, and pickled ginger get the sharp treatment.* Left: *Spoons dipped into chocolate are an elegant touch. Use them to stir spiced coffee and then say goodnight.*

Left: *Bubbly red shiraz adds sparkle and sophistication to a party, and all you have to do is chill the bottle, then open and pour.* Below: *Another easy treat. Bite-sized dark chocolate cups are filled with a selection of ice creams scooped with a melon baller. Simply buy the chocolate cups and some good-quality ice creams, combine them 2 days before the party, and serve straight from the freezer.*

fork

Stand up and be contented. This chapter is full of **tasty ideas** for parties where you want to **make a meal** of it. Knives get the **chop** when guests are not at table, so food has to sit easily on the fork and **stay there**, all the way into the mouth. You will want to offer choice along with the **heartwarming hospitality**, so **here is the scoop** on forkable meat, chicken, and fish dishes, plenty of pasta, **lots of rice**. There are terrific tarts, **salads** of all kinds, beans too. Desserts range from **unctuous** syllabubs to peachy-keen baked fruits, exotic ices, and **very necessary chocolate cake**. The feature pages in this section focus on the season of good cheer and **freewheeling** forky occasions such as **brunches** and picnics (there are chopsticks in those pictures, but you **get the idea**). Fill 'em up with dishes laid out on a **table** for guests to help themselves, or **serve** the food from a tray. A **buffet** by any other name would taste as sweet, but you can always skip the party and **eat this food** in front of the telly. **Bliss.**

FOOD

Roast beef salad

Most of the preparation for this rustic salad can be done well ahead, but don't slice the beef until just before serving. SERVES 10

5 large red bell peppers
4 red onions, sliced into ½-inch rounds
1½ tblsp olive oil
2½ lb beef tenderloin
1 tsp black peppercorns, lightly crushed
2 tblsp vegetable oil
1¼ cups (12 oz) sour cream
3 tblsp prepared horseradish
3 heads radicchio, torn into large pieces
1½ cups (12 oz) bottled artichokes
   in oil, drained
Salt & freshly ground pepper to taste

Broil the peppers until the skins are blackened. Place in a bowl, cover with plastic wrap, and let stand for 10 minutes.

Peel and seed the peppers and set the flesh aside to cool before chilling.

Put the onions in a single layer on a baking sheet, drizzle with olive oil, and season. Broil for about 6 minutes on one side or until they are slightly charred. Lift onto a plate to cool. Cover and chill.

Roll the beef in the crushed peppercorns.

Heat the vegetable oil in a roasting pan in an oven preheated to 425°F for 5 minutes or until very hot. Add the beef, sear it well on all sides, then roast for 15–20 minutes for rare, or 25–30 minutes for medium. Cool, cover, and chill.

Cut the beef into ¼-inch slices. Mix the sour cream and horseradish together to make a dressing, then season to taste. Cut the peppers into wide strips.

Arrange the radicchio, peppers, onion, beef, and artichokes on a dish. Spoon over some of the dressing and serve.

Advance preparation: Broil the peppers up to 3 days ahead, the beef up to 2 days ahead, and broil the onions and make the dressing up to 1 day ahead; cover and chill. Assemble 1 hour before, cover, and keep cool; dress just before serving.
Freezing: Not suitable.

left Saffron lamb tagine

Sticky gingered beef

Tossing the beef in sugar gives it a caramel taste and lovely rich color. SERVES 10

5 scallions, halved crosswise
2½ lb lean beef, cut into strips
¼ cup sugar
3¾ cups basmati rice
18–20 saffron threads
1 tblsp boiling water
¼ cup toasted sesame oil
for the sauce
¾ cup white wine vinegar
1¼ cup hoisin sauce
1 tblsp Worcestershire sauce
A few drops of Tabasco sauce
4 small pieces pickled ginger, finely
   chopped
Salt & freshly ground pepper to taste

Cut the scallions into long thin strips and put them into a bowl of ice water for about 20 minutes to crisp and curl.

Coat the beef with the sugar.

Wash the rice in several changes of water and drain well.

Mix the saffron with the boiling water and let stand for 10 minutes.

Boil the rice and saffron in a large pan of salted water for 8–10 minutes or until the rice is soft outside but firm inside. Drain, cover with foil, and keep warm.

Heat some of the sesame oil in a wok or heavy frying pan. Stir-fry the beef in batches for 3–5 minutes or until browned. Transfer each cooked batch to a plate.

Add the vinegar to the wok and simmer over high heat until it has reduced to about ¼ cup.

Lower the heat to medium and add the hoisin, Worcestershire and Tabasco sauces, and the chopped ginger. Season. When the sauce starts to bubble, add the beef and heat through for 2–3 minutes.

Drain and dry the scallions.

Spoon the hot rice and beef into separate serving dishes. Garnish the beef with the scallions and serve.

Advance preparation: Chop the ginger up to 2 days before, cover, and keep cool. Cut the scallions, place in ice water, cover, and chill; slice the beef, cover, and

chill up to 1 day ahead.
Freezing: Not suitable.

Saffron lamb tagine

Dates, prunes, and apricots can be used instead of raisins or cranberries. SERVES 10

18–20 saffron threads
1 tblsp boiling water
5 lb boneless stewing lamb, cut
   into large dice
¼ cup vegetable oil
1 lb cippolini, button, or pearl onions
1 large clove garlic, crushed
1 tsp ground ginger
A large pinch of cayenne pepper
½ tsp ground cinnamon
1 lb canned chopped tomatoes
5 cups chicken stock
2½ tblsp raisins
¾ cup unskinned almonds
2 tblsp butter
3 tblsp pistachios, skinned
3 tblsp dried cranberries

Preheat the oven to 375°F. Mix the saffron with the boiling water and let stand for 10 minutes.

Fry the lamb in batches in hot oil over high heat for 2–3 minutes to brown it on all sides. Remove with a slotted spoon and transfer to an ovenproof dish.

Pour off all but 1 tablespoon of the oil from the pan, lower the heat, and cook the onions in it for 4–5 minutes or until golden.

Stir in the garlic, spices, and saffron liquid and cook for 1 minute. Add the tomatoes, stock, and raisins. Bring to a boil and season well. Stir into the lamb, cover, and bake in the oven for 1½ hours or until tender.

Sauté the almonds in hot butter for 1–2 minutes, then add the pistachios, cranberries, and a large pinch of salt. Scatter over the lamb tagine and serve.

Advance preparation: Make up to 3 days ahead, cover, and cool. Reheat in a preheated oven at 375°F for 45–60 minutes or until piping hot.
Freezing: Freeze the cooked tagine up to 4 weeks before and reheat as above.

Chicken tonnato salad

Delicious though tuna sauce is in the classic Italian dish of vitello tonnato, it's also pretty wonderful with chicken. SERVES 10

Ten 6-oz boneless, skinless chicken
  breast halves
Oil for greasing
10 oz French beans or baby Blue Lake
  green beans
1 cup black olives
20 anchovies stuffed with capers
Salt & freshly ground pepper to taste
for the tuna sauce
Heaping ¼ cup mayonnaise
3 oz canned tuna in oil + 2 tblsp of
  the oil
1 heaping tblsp capers, drained
1 tblsp fresh lemon juice

Season and cook the chicken on a hot, lightly oiled ridged cast-iron grill pan for 8–10 minutes, turning once, or until cooked through. Remove, cool, and slice each chicken breast into 6 pieces.
Cook the beans in boiling salted water for 3–5 minutes or until crisp-tender. Drain in a colander, then plunge into cold water until cold to retain the color. Drain.
Dry the beans on paper towels, then cut them in half lengthwise.

Put the mayonnaise in a blender or processor and blend with the tuna, oil, capers, lemon juice, and pepper until smooth.
Arrange the chicken on a serving dish and drizzle over the tuna sauce. Place the beans, olives, and the stuffed anchovies on top and serve.

Advance preparation: Make the sauce up to 2 days before and grill the chicken and cook the beans up to 1 day ahead; cover and chill. Assemble up to 1 hour before, cover, and chill.
Freezing: Not suitable.

Vietnamese chicken salad

This is a sensational salad — light, pretty, and with a distinctive, fresh-tasting sauce. The sauce, nuoc cham, is Vietnam's equivalent of the soy sauce of China and Japan, in that it's liberally used in cooking and as an accompaniment to food. SERVES 10

Ten 6-oz boneless, skinless chicken
  breast halves
1 cup water
¼ cup dry white wine
3 tblsp olive oil
1 bay leaf

8 black peppercorns
12 oz carrot
12 oz cucumber
12 oz daikon
1½ cups bean sprouts
1½ cups shredded Napa cabbage
2 oz mixed Asian salad greens, such
  as mizuna & tat soi
½ cup mint leaves
½ cup cilantro leaves
Salt to taste
for the nuoc cham dressing
¼ cup fresh lime juice
3 tblsp Thai fish sauce
3 tblsp rice vinegar
3 tblsp vegetable oil
2 tblsp palm sugar or dark brown sugar
1 hot red chili, seeded & finely chopped
2 cloves garlic, crushed

Combine all the dressing ingredients and let sit for 30 minutes.
Heat the oven to 375°F. Put the chicken, water, wine, oil, bay leaf, peppercorns, and some salt into a roasting pan. Cover with foil and bake for about 15–20 minutes or until cooked through.
Remove the chicken from the oven, drain, and cool on paper towels. Slice each breast into 8 pieces.
Cut the carrots and cucumber into chunky pieces. Shave the radish into very fine ribbons using a vegetable peeler.
Toss the chicken, vegetables, salad greens, and herbs together in the dressing, arrange on a platter and serve.

Advance preparation: Make the dressing and cook the chicken up to 2 days before. Prepare the carrots and radish and put into water, and prepare the cucumber up to 1 day ahead; cover and chill. Assemble up to 1 hour before, cover, and chill.
Freezing: Not suitable.

Chicken tonnato salad

right Vietnamese chicken salad

Chicken scaloppine with mozzarella & sage

Chicken layered with mozzarella cheese, paper-thin prosciutto, and a sliver of pungent garlic and quickly fried in olive oil is my idea of food heaven. SERVES 10

Ten 6-oz boneless, skinless chicken
  breast halves, each cut into 4 pieces
10 slices prosciutto di Parma, halved
  crosswise
4 balls mozzarella, each cut into 5 pieces
4 cloves garlic, each cut into 5 pieces
20 sage leaves
¾ cup olive oil
3 cups red cherry tomatoes
3 cups yellow cherry tomatoes
1¼ cups dry white wine
2 cups chicken stock
Salt & freshly ground pepper to taste

Flatten each piece of chicken between 2 sheets of plastic wrap with a rolling pin until about doubled in size, around 2½ inches in diameter and ¼ inch thick. Season well.

Divide the prosciutto, mozzarella, and garlic among 20 of the chicken pieces. Top with the remaining chicken and press a sage leaf on top.

Preheat the oven to 375°F. Put the cherry tomatoes into a roasting pan with 2 tablespoons of the olive oil, season, and roast for 10 minutes.

Add some of the remaining oil to a large pan and fry the chicken in batches, leaf side down first, over medium heat for 3 minutes on each side. Remove the chicken, cover, and keep warm while frying the rest.

Pour the wine into the pan and let it simmer for 1 minute before adding the stock and bringing it to a boil. Cook until reduced by a third, then season.

Return the scaloppine to the pan, lower the heat to a simmer, and heat through for 2 minutes. Serve, sage leaves uppermost, with the roasted tomatoes.

Advance preparation: Prepare the chicken to the point of cooking up to 1 day before, cover, and chill. Cook the chicken and tomatoes to order.
Freezing: Not suitable.

Butter chicken masala

A wonderfully hot but beautifully creamy chicken dish. If you can't stand hot food, halve, or even quarter, the amount of chili powder used. Serve the curry with lots of plain steamed basmati rice and a glass of Coconut Cooler (page 152). Do not be deterred by the long list of ingredients in this recipe, as most of them are commonly used spices. SERVES 10

6 lb boneless, skinless chicken

for the marinade

1 cup (8 oz) plain yogurt
1 tblsp olive oil
2 tblsp fresh lemon juice
1 tsp ground turmeric
2 tsp garam masala
1 tblsp hot chili powder
2 tsp ground cumin
2 tsp finely grated fresh ginger

2 large cloves garlic, crushed
2 tsp salt

for the sauce

¾ cup cashew nuts
1 large onion, finely chopped
¼ cup olive oil
1 clove garlic, crushed
1 tblsp finely grated fresh ginger
1¼ cups water
⅔ cup tomato paste

2 tblsp honey
¼ cup heavy cream
1 bay leaf
5 curry leaves + extra for garnishing
A large pinch of fenugreek
A large pinch of ground cardamom
2 tsp garam masala
2 tblsp butter
1 tblsp cardamom pods
Salt to taste

Cut the chicken into large pieces.
Mix all the marinade ingredients together, coat the chicken with this mixture, cover, and marinate for 8 hours in the fridge.
Preheat the oven to 400°F. Divide the marinated chicken between 2 roasting pans and bake in the hot oven for 15 minutes.
Process half the cashew nuts in a blender or processor for 1 minute to make a paste.
Fry the onion in oil in a large frying pan over medium heat for 5–7 minutes or until soft and golden brown. Add the garlic and ginger and cook for 1 minute.
Stir in the cashew paste, water, tomato paste, honey, cream, bay leaf, the 5 curry leaves, fenugreek, ground cardamom, and garam masala. Mix well, bring to a boil, lower the heat, and simmer for 10 minutes or until the sauce has thickened to a coating consistency.
Sauté the cardamom pods and remaining cashew nuts quickly in the butter for 1–2 minutes.
Transfer the cooked chicken from the oven to the pan of sauce and simmer for 10 minutes, making sure that each piece of chicken is well coated.
Spoon the mixture into a serving dish, scatter over the sautéed cashews and cardamom, and garnish with the remaining curry leaves. Serve hot.

Advance preparation: Make the sauce up to 4 days before and cook the chicken in the sauce up to 2 days before; cover and chill. Reheat in a preheated 375°F oven for 30–40 minutes or until piping hot.
Freezing: Freeze the marinated chicken and the sauce separately up to 4 weeks before. Freeze the cooked chicken in the sauce up to 3 weeks before and reheat as above.

left Butter chicken masala

Red duck curry

It should take you about 45 minutes from start to finish to make this fragrant duck curry from Southeast Asia. If you want to add some vegetables, sautéed eggplant and shallots would do the job nicely. Plain steamed jasmine rice is the best accompaniment. SERVES 10

2⅓ cups jasmine rice
Ten 8-oz duck breasts
¼ cup Thai red curry paste
2 stalks lemongrass, finely chopped (white part only)
8 kaffir lime leaves + extra for garnishing
1 large hot red chili, halved & seeded + extra whole chilies for garnishing
1¼ cups coconut milk
1¼ cups duck or chicken stock
Salt & freshly ground pepper to taste

Wash the rice in several changes of cold water and drain well.
Remove the skin and fat from the duck and put them into a large pan. Cook over medium heat to melt the fat. Reserve 3 tablespoons of this fat in the pan.
Cook the rice in a large pan of boiling unsalted water for 8 minutes. Lower the heat and cook for 3 minutes more or until the rice is no longer chalky in the center. Drain, cover, and keep warm.
Slice each duck breast into 8 pieces and stir-fry them in the duck fat in batches over high heat for about 3 minutes per batch. Return all the meat to the pan.
Add the curry paste, lemongrass, lime leaves, and chili to the pan and cook for 1 minute over medium heat. Stir in the coconut milk and stock. Cover, reduce the heat to low, and simmer for 10 minutes or until the duck is tender.
Garnish the curry with the extra lime leaves and chilies and serve with the cooked jasmine rice.

Advance preparation: Make the curry up to 8 hours ahead, cover, and chill. Reheat gently for about 10 minutes or until hot. Cook the rice up to 1 hour ahead, cover with foil, and keep warm in a 275°F oven.
Freezing: Not suitable.

Seared salmon, asparagus & potato salad

A very English salad that is best made with new season's salmon, potatoes, and asparagus. Ideally, serve it slightly warm, but if that's not possible, serve it cold and make sure that you take it out of the fridge a good 30 minutes beforehand. Finish the meal with a bowl of jewel-bright Red Berry Kissel (page 132) and some crème fraîche. SERVES 10

2¼ lb unpeeled small new waxy potatoes
1¾ salmon fillet, boned and skinned
1 tblsp olive oil + extra for greasing
2 tsp fine sea salt
½ tsp paprika
12 oz asparagus, each spear cut
   diagonally into 3
1 heaping tblsp finely chopped
   fresh chervil leaves
1 heaping tblsp finely chopped
   fresh mint leaves
1 heaping tblsp finely chopped
   fresh basil leaves
Salt & freshly ground pepper to taste
for the mustard dressing
1 tblsp sweet mustard
2 tblsp olive oil
¼ cup fresh lemon juice
1½ tsp sugar

Whisk all the dressing ingredients together and season to taste.

Seared salmon, asparagus & potato salad

Cook the potatoes in boiling salted water for 10–12 minutes or until tender.
Drain, cool a little, cut in half, then pour over half the mustard dressing and toss well. The potatoes will absorb more flavor if you do this while they are hot.
Rub the salmon on both sides, first with the oil and then with a mixture of the salt and paprika.
Sear the fish on a very hot, oiled ridged cast-iron grill pan on both sides for a total of 8–10 minutes or until crisp and golden on the outside and still slightly pink in the middle. Transfer to a tray to cool. Break into neat, forkable pieces.
Boil the asparagus for about 3 minutes in a pan of salted water or until al dente. Drain in a colander under running cold water to preserve the color, then dry on paper towels. Alternatively, cook the spears on the grill pan for 4–5 minutes.
Arrange the potatoes, salmon, and asparagus in a dish. Drizzle over the remaining dressing and scatter over a mixture of the fresh herbs. Serve.

Advance preparation: Make the dressing up to 2 days before and cook the salmon, potatoes, and asparagus up to 1 day ahead; cover and chill. Assemble up to 4 hours before, except for the herbs, cover, and chill. Remove from the fridge 30 minutes before serving and

scatter over the herbs.
Freezing: Not suitable.

Zucchini & seafood salad

Tossed in a refreshing lemon and olive oil dressing, this salad of scallops, shrimp, squid, paper-thin raw zucchini, and a few leaves is ideal served as part of a buffet or on its own. Squid goes through three stages of cooking: tender, tough, tender. To get the best results, it needs to be cooked briefly for 1 or 2 minutes, or for a long time, as anything in between makes it rubbery. SERVES 10

20 bay scallops
½ cup lemon olive oil or extra-
   virgin olive oil
1 lb squid, cut into fine rings
1 clove garlic, crushed
2 tblsp fresh lemon juice
20 large shrimp, cooked, shelled,
   and deveined
3 cups baby spinach
5 oz baby zucchini, very finely sliced
2 heaping tblsp minced fresh chervil
Salt & freshly ground pepper to taste

Sauté the scallops in batches in 2 tablespoons of the oil over high heat for 1–2 minutes or until just cooked. Remove from the pan and set aside.
Cook the squid and garlic in batches in another 2 tablespoons of the oil over high heat for 1–2 minutes or until opaque and tender.
Let the scallops and squid cool.
Whisk the remaining oil with the lemon juice and some seasoning.
Put all the salad ingredients, except for the chervil, in a bowl and lightly toss in the lemon dressing. Scatter over the chervil leaves and serve.

Advance preparation: Cook the scallops and squid, crush the garlic, slice the zucchini, and make the lemon dressing up to 6 hours before; cover and chill. Assemble up to 30 minutes ahead.

right Zucchini & seafood salad

Thai mussels

These steamed mussels, in a refreshing aromatic Thai broth, give their French counterpart, moules marinière, a good run for their money. SERVES 10

6 stalks lemongrass, white part only
4 tomatoes
2¼ cups water
6 cloves garlic, crushed
1 lb Thai red or French shallots, halved
One 4-inch piece galangal or root ginger, sliced
10 lb mussels, scrubbed and debearded
1 tsp red chili flakes
2 large fresh hot green chilies, seeded
¼ cup Thai fish sauce
2 tblsp palm sugar or dark brown sugar

Pound the lemongrass with a pestle or mallet to crush.

Put the tomatoes in a bowl, pour over boiling water to cover, and let sit for about 10 seconds. Plunge them into cold water, peel off the skin, then quarter the tomatoes and remove and discard the seeds. Coarsely chop the tomato flesh.

Divide the 2½ cups water, lemongrass, garlic, shallots, and galangal or ginger between 2 large pans. Bring to a boil. Divide the tomatoes, chili flakes, fresh chilies, fish sauce, sugar, and mussels between these pans.

Cover and cook over high heat for 4–5 minutes or until all the mussels have opened. Discard any that have not, along with the lemongrass stalks.

Transfer the mussels and vegetable broth to bowls and serve.

Advance preparation: Prepare the tomatoes up to 4 hours before, cover, and chill. Cook the mussels to order.
Freezing: Not suitable.

Bruschetta with red snapper, fried crumbs & capers

Crisp bruschetta oozing with olive oil, draped with red snapper fillets, and scattered with fried crumbs make a tasty first course or main course. Some arugula leaves would be an attractive and delicious accompaniment. SERVES 10

Ten 3-oz red snapper fillets
1¼ cups dry white wine
2 tsp hot red chili flakes
2 tsp fine sea salt
2½ cups coarse bread crumbs
4 tblsp olive oil
2 heaping tblsp capers preserved in balsamic vinegar, drained
Ten ½-inch slices ciabatta bread
Lemon olive oil or extra-virgin olive oil for drizzling
1 heaping tblsp chopped fresh parsley
5 small lemons, halved lengthwise

Preheat the oven to 375°F. Put the red snapper skin side up in a roasting pan with the white wine. Sprinkle over the chili flakes and salt.

Roast in the oven for 8–10 minutes or until cooked. Drain on paper towels.

Fry the bread crumbs in 2 tablespoons of the olive oil over medium heat, stirring constantly, for 2–3 minutes or until crisp and golden. Add the capers during the last minute of frying. Keep warm.

Grill the ciabatta bread on both sides in a very hot ridged cast-iron grill pan until crisp, or toast under a preheated broiler. Drizzle the bread with the remaining 2 tablespoons of olive oil.

Place a roasted snapper fillet on top of each slice of toasted bread, then spoon over the fried crumbs and capers.

Drizzle with the lemon olive oil or extra-virgin oil and garnish with the chopped parsley and a lemon half. Serve the bruschetta warm or hot.

Advance preparation: Fry the crumbs up to 2 days ahead and cover. Chop the parsley up to 1 day before, cover, and chill. Reheat the crumbs in a pan with the capers for 1 minute. Cook the snapper and bruschetta to order.
Freezing: Freeze the fried crumbs up to 4 weeks in advance.

Bruschetta with red snapper, fried crumbs & capers

left Thai mussels

the menu

Grissini & rouille dip

Bacon & egg linguine

Green salad

Red berry kissel with biscotti & vanilla cream

Cheese & fresh figs

Oyster shooters

Lime, orange & lemon citrus pressés

brunch

Clockwise from top right:
*Bacon and eggs are perfect
morning food and delicious mixed
with pasta and herbs; a luscious
fruity conclusion, Red Berry
Kissel can be used in myriad
ways but here it is simply served
with flavored cream; brunch is
casual so guests will be happy to
see you preparing the food and
may even want to help;
indispensable Green Salad with
balsamic dressing.*

Below: *Serve the Lime, Orange & Lemon Citrus Pressés in colorful tumblers to complement the flavors of the drink and garnish with contrasting twists of peel.* Right: *A whole fine cheese served with baguette or rustic sourdough, mounds of crunchy walnuts still in their shells, and fresh summery figs. Shopping is the only preparation required, and guests can serve themselves.*

Top: *These grissini are made from a simple bread recipe, then rolled with flavorings such as olives, red chili, sea salt, and herbs before baking. Serve them with a spicy rouille for dipping, made by your own hand or bought from a good store if time is tight.* Left: *Oyster Shooters are a glamorous alternative to the traditional brunchtime bloody Marys and an excellent wake-up call for any guests who are still feeling sleepy.*

Scrambled eggs with garlic & thyme

These creamy scrambled eggs are flavored with garlic and thyme and then piled back in their shells. Suitable for brunches, lunches, and suppers, serve them with some home-made grissini for dipping. SERVES 10

14 large eggs
3 large cloves garlic, cut into 20 slices
2 tsp olive oil
6 tblsp unsalted butter
¼ cup heavy cream
10 sprigs thyme
Grissini (page 37)
Salt & freshly ground pepper to taste

Cut the tops off the eggs with a serrated knife and pour the yolks and whites into a bowl. Wash and dry 10 of the best eggshells and put them into egg cups.
Fry the garlic in oil over medium heat for 5–7 minutes or until crisp and golden. Drain on paper towels.
Pass the eggs through a sieve to remove the stringy bits.
Melt the butter in a small, heavy pan over very low heat, add the eggs, and stir constantly for about 3–5 minutes or until they are creamy with light curds and just hold their shape.
Remove from the heat; stir in the cream and seasoning. Transfer to a bowl, otherwise the eggs will keep on cooking.
Spoon the scrambled eggs into the eggshells, top with the garlic and thyme, and serve with the grissini.

Advance preparation: Prepare the eggshells and fry the garlic up to 1 day before; cover.
Freezing: Not suitable.

left Scrambled eggs with garlic & thyme

Fried Mexican eggs with chorizo & spicy salsa

Fried Mexican eggs with chorizo & spicy salsa

These Mexican eggs, perfect for brunches, call out to be served with an icy-cold glass of beer. SERVES 10

10 slices bread
8 oz chorizo, cut into 30 slices
Vegetable oil or frying
10 medium eggs
Salt & freshly ground pepper to taste
for the spicy salsa
5 Roma (plum) tomatoes
5 tblsp tomato purée
3 tblsp chopped fresh cilantro
2 large hot red chilies, seeded & coarsely chopped
2 tblsp olive oil
1 clove garlic, crushed
You will also need a 3-inch round cutter

Cut out rounds from the center of each slice of bread, using the cutter.
Put the tomatoes in a bowl, pour over boiling water to cover, and let stand for about 10 seconds. Plunge them into cold water, peel, quarter, and discard the seeds.
Chop the tomato flesh coarsely and mix it with the tomato purée, chili, and cilantro to make the salsa.

Heat the olive oil over low heat, add the garlic, fry for 1 minute, add the tomato mixture, and heat until the salsa is hot, about 5 minutes. Season.
Fry the chorizo in a very hot frying pan for 30 seconds on each side, or until heated through. Cover and keep warm.
Heat the vegetable oil in a large frying pan and fry the bread in batches over medium heat on one side only until crisp.
Turn the bread over and put it back in the pan, again in batches.
Crack an egg into the middle of each piece of bread and fry for 2–3 minutes, spooning hot oil over the top of the eggs to cook them.
Season the eggs, transfer to plates, spoon over the salsa, and arrange a few slices of chorizo on the side. Serve.

Advance preparation: Cut the bread out, prepare the salsa up the point of cooking, and slice the chorizo up to 1 day before. Cover and chill. Fry the chorizo, bread, and eggs to order. Heat the salsa as above.
Freezing: Not suitable.

Gruyère, artichoke & mortadella tart

This mix of artichokes, sautéed mortadella, and Gruyère in a rosemary custard makes a distinctive, rustic, and well-flavored tart.
SERVES 10

½ recipe Savory Pastry (page 57)
Flour for rolling
for the filling
10 oz mortadella, cut into
  1-inch pieces
1 tblsp olive oil
1¼ cups bottled artichokes in oil,
  drained and halved
1½ cups (6 oz) shredded Gruyère cheese
1¼ cups heavy cream
3 large eggs
1 large egg yolk

1 tblsp finely chopped fresh rosemary
Salt & freshly ground pepper to taste
You will also need a 10-inch shallow false-bottomed fluted tart pan, parchment paper, and dried beans or pie weights.

Roll the chilled pastry thinly on a lightly floured surface to a circle 2 inches larger than the pan. Wrap the pastry around the rolling pin and let it unroll over the pan, pressing it down into the bottom and up the sides. Roll the pin over the top of the pan to trim away any excess pastry and give a clean edge. Lightly prick the base with a fork and chill for 30 minutes.
Fry the mortadella in hot oil over medium heat for 4–5 minutes or until evenly browned. Drain on paper towels.

Gruyère, artichoke & mortadella tart

Preheat the oven to 400°F.
Line the tart with parchment paper and dried beans or pie weights and bake the pastry for 15 minutes. Remove the paper and beans or weights and bake 5 minutes more or until golden. Cool a little.
Arrange the mortadella, artichokes, and cheese in the bottom of the tart shell.
Whisk together the cream, eggs, yolk, rosemary, and seasoning. Pour into the tart and bake in the hot oven for 20 minutes, or until the custard has set.
Cool the tart for 10 minutes before transferring it from the pan to a serving dish. Serve hot or cold.

Advance preparation: Bake the tart shell, fry the mortadella, and make the custard up to 1 day before; store the tart shell in an airtight container; cover and chill the mortadella and custard. Bake to order if serving hot, allowing an extra 5 minutes cooking time. If serving cold, bake up to 12 hours ahead, cover, and chill. Remove from the fridge 1 hour before serving.
Freezing: The tart can be frozen unbaked in its pan for up to 1 week and baked straight from the freezer. Freeze it baked up to 3 weeks ahead.

Tomato & pesto galettes

Stunningly easy to make, particularly if you choose to buy both the pastry and the pesto, this galette is a good do-ahead recipe when time is short. Substitute tapenade for pesto if you prefer. Serve at brunches or suppers, with the Arugula, French Bean, Red Onion & Croûton Salad (page 128). SERVES 10

2½ lb puff pastry
Flour for dusting
Butter for greasing
5 recipes Chunky Pesto (page 43), or
  1⅔ cups ready-made pesto
10 Roma (plum) tomatoes, thinly sliced
3 tblsp olive oil
10 basil sprigs
Salt & freshly ground pepper to taste

Roll the pastry out on a lightly floured surface to ⅛ inch thick. Cut out ten 6½-inch circles using a small plate as a template. Transfer them to 4 lightly greased baking sheets, prick with a fork, and chill for 30 minutes.

Preheat the oven to 400°F. Bake the pastries in batches for 8–10 minutes or until golden. Switch the pans in the oven halfway through cooking.

Divide the pesto among the pastry galettes, spreading it to the edges. Arrange the tomatoes on top, drizzle with the oil, and season.

Broil under a preheated broiler for 1–2 minutes or until the tomatoes have softened a little and the pastry is warmed through. Garnish with the basil and serve.

Advance preparation: Bake the pastries up to 1 day before and store in an airtight container. Assemble up to 2 hours before and grill to order, allowing an extra 2 minutes for grilling.
Freezing: The baked pastries can be frozen up to 3 weeks ahead. Defrost and grill for an extra 2 minutes.

Polenta, Taleggio & wild mushrooms

Polenta taragna is a mixture of polenta and buckwheat flour with a speckled appearance. Adding masses of Taleggio and butter makes it very creamy and rich, while the garlicky mushrooms improve it some more! This is a wintry, stick-to-the-ribs dish. SERVES 10

for the polenta
9 cups water
2 tsp salt
4 cups (1 lb) polenta taragna or
    regular polenta
¾ cup (1½ sticks) + 2 tblsp butter
1 lb taleggio cheese, rind removed, diced
Freshly ground pepper to taste
for the wild mushrooms
1½ lb mixed wild mushrooms,
    such as porcini, chanterelles, and
    stemmed shiitakes
2 large cloves garlic, crushed
¼ cup olive oil
4 tblsp butter
Salt & freshly ground pepper to taste

Tomato & pesto galette

Bring the water and salt to a boil in a large pan, reduce the heat to a simmer, and very slowly pour in the polenta, whisking all the while to prevent lumps.

Mix in half the butter and continue to cook the polenta over low heat, stirring constantly with a wooden spoon for 20–25 minutes. The polenta is ready when it is smooth, thick, and comes away from the side of the pan.

Sauté the mushrooms and garlic in the oil and butter in batches over a high heat for 4–5 minutes or until tender. Season thoroughly.

Remove the polenta from the heat. Stir in the cheese, the rest of the butter, and the pepper. Mix well and transfer to a serving dish. Spoon over the cooked mushrooms and any juices. Serve.

Advance preparation: Sauté the mushrooms up to 2 hours before and cover. Quickly sauté for 3–4 minutes to reheat. Make the polenta to order.
Freezing: Not suitable.

Tabbouleh primavera

Serve this tabbouleh as a light first course or as an accompaniment to the Zucchini & Seafood Salad (page 100). It also makes a good canapé filling when served in hollowed-out cucumber cups, but you will need to cut the vegetables smaller. SERVES 10

1⅓ cups bulgur wheat
1½ cups boiling water
Grated zest & juice of 3 lemons
4½ tblsp olive oil
2½ lb fava beans, shelled
1 lb thin asparagus
¾ cup bean sprouts
1 cup thinly sliced scallions
2 heaping tblsp finely chopped fresh mint
1 heaping tblsp finely chopped fresh chervil
Salt & freshly ground pepper to taste

Put the bulgur in a bowl with the boiling water, lemon juice, and oil. Mix well, cover, and let sit 1 hour or until the grains soak up all the liquid.

Cook the fava beans and asparagus separately in pans of boiling salted water for 3 minutes.

Drain and refresh the fava beans and asparagus under running cold water until cold to stop the cooking process and preserve the color. Dry on paper towels.

Cut the asparagus in half lengthwise and then diagonally in half again. Peel and discard the outer skins of the fava beans.

Season the bulgur with salt and pepper, then add all the vegetables, plus most of the lemon zest, mint leaves, and chervil, and toss gently.

Transfer the mixture to a salad bowl. Scatter over the remaining zest, mint, and chervil, and serve.

Advance preparation: Cook and refresh the fava beans and asparagus, slice the scallions, zest and squeeze the lemons up to 1 day ahead; cover and chill. Soak the bulgur wheat up to 8 hours before, but you may need to add some extra oil and lemon juice if it becomes too dry. Cover and chill. Assemble up to 1 hour before.
Freezing: Not suitable.

Tabbouleh primavera

Wild & red Camargue rice salad with blood oranges & grilled red onions

Wild & red Camargue rice salad with blood oranges & grilled red onions

Apart from the interesting mix of flavors and textures in this Mediterranean-inspired salad, the range of red colors, from the bold scarlet radishes to the more muted tones of the grilled red onions, make it a striking dish for a summer buffet table. SERVES 10

for the salad

Scant 1 cup wild rice

Scant 1 cup red Camargue or
   other red rice

3 small red onions, cut into ½-inch
   slices

2 tblsp olive oil

5 blood oranges

½ cucumber, cut into irregular chunks

1 head radicchio

1 bunch radishes, halved through
   the stalks

Salt & freshly ground pepper to taste

for the citrus dressing

⅓ cup olive oil

1 tblsp white wine vinegar

1 tsp balsamic vinegar

4½ tblsp orange juice

Salt & freshly ground pepper to taste

Cook the wild rice in a pan of salted boiling water for 25 minutes or until al dente. Drain in a colander, refresh under cold water, and drain again.

Boil the red rice in another pan of boiling salted water for 20 minutes and drain and refresh as above. Do not cook both varieties of rice together, as the red rice will stain the wild rice and you will lose the distinct color of each.

Preheat the broiler to the highest setting. Put the red onions in a single layer on a baking sheet, drizzle over the olive oil, and season.

Broil the onions for about 6 minutes on one side only until they are slightly

charred at the edges. Remove from the heat and transfer to a plate to cool.

Prepare the blood oranges by cutting a slice from the top and bottom of each with a small sharp knife. Carve away the peel and pith, following the curve of the fruit, leaving the flesh exposed. Slice into ¼-inch circles, flicking out any seeds.

Trim the base of the radicchio to separate all the leaves and then cut each leaf lengthwise into ⅛-inch-wide strips.

Whisk all the ingredients for the dressing together in a small bowl and season.

Toss the wild and red rices together in the dressing and season. Mix in the remaining salad ingredients and serve.

Advance preparation: Up to 1 day ahead, cook both kinds of rice, grill the onions, slice the oranges, and make the dressing; cover and chill. Assemble up to 2 hours before.
Freezing: Not suitable.

Persian jeweled rice

Dramatic in its brilliant colors from saffron, barberries, and pistachios, this elegant Persian jeweled rice can be served as a main course, or with a simple roast chicken dish. Barberries, once used in cooking in medieval England, are available from Iranian food shops, where they are sold dried and known as zereshk. They have a very tart flavor and need to be stemmed and rinsed before use. This dish can also be served cold. SERVES 10

1½ cups basmati rice
18–20 saffron threads
1 tblsp boiling water
1 heaping tsp cardamom pods
1 heaping tsp coriander seeds
3 tblsp olive oil
3 tblsp dried barberries
½ cup dried cranberries
⅔ cup raisins
⅔ cup pistachio nuts, skinned
Salt & freshly ground pepper to taste

Wash the rice in several changes of cold water and drain well. Mix the saffron with the boiling water and let stand for 10 minutes.

Add the rice to a large pan of salted boiling water with the cardamom and coriander. Bring it back to a boil and boil for 8–10 minutes or until the rice is soft on the outside but still firm in the center. Drain in a colander.

Put the oil in a large pan over medium heat. Add the barberries, cranberries, raisins, and pistachios and sauté for 1 minute to plump up the fruits. Stir in the rice and the saffon liquid, season well, and stir until piping hot. Serve.

Advance preparation: Only if serving cold, make the jeweled rice up to 1 day before, cover, and chill. Do not reheat cooked rice.
Freezing: Not suitable.

left Persian jeweled rice

Lemon & beet risottos

Not only are these two risottos on a plate striking to look at, they both taste wonderful in their own right. The lemon version partners fish extremely well, while the sweet flavor of beet is a good accompaniment to game and smoked sausages. Risottos cannot be rushed; you need to stand at the stove stirring and adding hot stock all the time so that the rice slowly absorbs all the liquid. That is the secret of good risotto. SERVES 10

for the beet risotto

8 oz raw beets
Vegetable oil for deep-frying
3 cups vegetable or chicken stock
2 tblsp olive oil
4 tblsp butter
1 onion, finely chopped
scant 1 cup Arborio or Carnaroli rice
1¼ cups dry red wine

for the lemon risotto

6 cups vegetable or chicken stock
2 tblsp olive oil
4 tblsp butter
1 onion, finely chopped
1½ cups arborio or carnaroli rice
⅔ cup dry white wine
Grated zest & juice of 4 lemons
¼ cup mascarpone
Salt & freshly ground pepper to taste
Grated Parmesan cheese

Cut 10 thin slices from the beets and shred the rest. Heat some oil for deep-frying to 400°F and fry the sliced beet for about 30 seconds or until crisp. Drain the beet crisps on paper towels and lightly salt.

Heat both quantities of stock in a pan and keep warm over low heat.

Put the olive oil, half the butter and the onions for both risottos in a heavy pan over low heat and sauté until soft and translucent, 8–10 minutes.

Add both quantities of rice, increase the heat to medium and stir well to make sure the rice is evenly coated with oil and butter. Remove from the heat.

Transfer about a third of the rice mixture to another pan over medium heat, add the red wine, and let it evaporate before adding any stock. Stir in the shredded beet.

Put the second pan, containing the remaining two thirds of the rice mixture, back on medium heat, add the white wine, and let it evaporate. Stir in the lemon juice and half the lemon zest, reserving the rest to use as a garnish.

Bring the pan of stock to a low boil and keep it simmering while making the risottos. Start adding the hot stock to both pans, a ladleful at a time, stirring constantly, for 15–20 minutes. The beet risotto will need about half the amount that the lemon risotto uses. Make sure that each ladle of stock is completely absorbed before adding any more and that the rice is always just covered with liquid. When cooked, the rice should be tender on the outside but with a firm bite on the inside. The risotto should have a soft and runny consistency.

Season well. Beat the remaining butter into both risottos and add the mascarpone to the lemon risotto.

Put a spoonful of each risotto on a plate. Garnish each with a beet crisp and some of the reserved lemon zest. Serve immediately, with grated Parmesan.

Advance preparation: Fry the beet crisps and store in an airtight container, and grate the beet and sauté the onions; cover and chill up to 1 day before. Heat the onion before adding the rice. Zest and juice the lemons up to 4 hours before, cover, and chill. Make the risottos to order.
Freezing: Not suitable.

Lemon & beet risottos

Jambalaya

This peppery Cajun dish, derived from Spanish paella, is among my favorite one-pot dishes. As I always have rice, onions, garlic, and some sort of salami in my pantry, it's a good dish for impromptu entertaining. Any missing vegetables are substituted for with whatever I happen to have in the fridge. SERVES 10

1½ cups red Camargue or other red rice
1½ cups long-grain white rice
1 large onion, coarsely chopped
3 cloves garlic, crushed
¾ cup olive oil
3 yellow or red bell peppers, seeded &
  cut into chunky pieces
12 oz chorizo or other spicy sausage,
  cut into ½-inch slices
12 oz white mushrooms
1 lb medium shrimp, shelled
  and deveined
3 cups chicken stock
2 tblsp chopped fresh thyme
Salt & freshly ground pepper to taste

Boil the red rice in a pan of boiling salted water for about 30 minutes and the long-grain rice in a separate pan for 10–12 minutes. When cooked, both should still have a little bite to them. Drain in a colander.

Fry the onion and garlic in 2 tablespoons of the oil in a large frying pan over medium heat for 4–5 minutes. Add the peppers, cook for 3 minutes, and then transfer the pan's contents to a bowl.

Sauté the chorizo over high heat for 1 minute, stirring all the time, and add to the onion mixture.

Pour half of the remaining oil into the pan and sauté the mushrooms over high heat for 2–3 minutes. Remove with a slotted spoon and add to the bowl.

Sauté the shrimp very quickly in the remaining oil, still over high heat, for 1–3 minutes or until pink. Remove and add to the other ingredients.

Put the stock in the pan, bring to a boil, then stir in the rice and the rest of the

left Jambalaya

ingredients, including the thyme. Heat the jambalaya for 5–6 minutes or until hot. Season well before serving.

Advance preparation: Sauté the onions, garlic, peppers, and mushrooms and chop the thyme up to 1 day before; cover and chill. Make the jambalaya to order. *Freezing: Not suitable.*

Scallop & cilantro kedgeree

Traditionally, kedgeree, also known as khichri, was an Indian mixture of leftover rice or lentils with onions and spices. British colonials then added haddock and it became a classic English breakfast dish. My version has those tiny slate-colored French lentils, seared scallops, and a handful of cilantro. Make it for brunch, lunch, or supper and serve with a green salad. SERVES 10

1½ cups Puy (green) lentils
2½ cups basmati rice
30 bay scallops
¼ cup olive oil
1 large onion, sliced
4 tblsp butter
1 heaping tsp ground cumin
1 heaping tsp garam masala
2½ cups fish or chicken stock
2 tblsp chopped fresh cilantro
4 hard-boiled eggs, coarsely chopped
10 lemon wedges
Mango chutney to serve
Salt & freshly ground pepper to taste

Put the lentils in a bowl, cover with boiling water, and let soak for 2 hours. Drain, transfer to a pan of fresh water, and boil for about 15–20 minutes or until tender. Drain again.
Wash the rice in several changes of cold water and drain well.
Sauté the scallops in batches in hot oil over high heat for 1–2 minutes or until just cooked.
Fry the onion in butter in a large saucepan over low heat for 5–6 minutes, stirring often. Raise the heat to medium and cook for 10–12 minutes or until brown and crispy.

Scallop & cilantro kedgeree

Stir in the cumin and garam masala and cook for 1 minute. Add the rice and stock, bring to a boil, stir, and cover.
Reduce the heat to low and cook for 10 minutes, by which time most of the liquid will have been absorbed.
Mix in the lentils, cilantro, and scallops and heat through for 3–4 minutes or until hot. Season well and serve, garnished

with chopped egg and lemon wedges. Serve with mango chutney.

Advance preparation: Cook the lentils, fry the onions, hard-boil the eggs, and chop the cilantro up to 1 day before; cover and chill. Make the kedgeree to order.
Freezing: Not suitable.

Penne with tomatoes & basil gremolata

This simple pasta salad is for serious garlic lovers. Using really good olive oil makes a big difference to the end result. Here I serve it cold, but there's no reason why it can't be served hot. SERVES 10

10 Roma (plum) tomatoes
¾ cup basil leaves, torn
Grated zest of 5 lemons
5 cloves garlic, finely chopped
1 tsp fine sea salt
1½ lb penne or similar pasta shape
¾ cup extra-virgin olive oil
3 heaping tblsp capers in balsamic
  vinegar, drained
Freshly ground pepper to taste

Put the tomatoes into a bowl, pour over boiling water to cover, and leave for 10 seconds. Plunge them into cold water, peel off the skins, quarter, then remove and discard the seeds. Coarsely chop the tomato flesh.
Mix the basil, lemon zest, garlic, and salt together for the gremolata.
Cook the pasta in a large pan of salted boiling water for 7–10 minutes or until al dente. Drain, rinse quickly under running cold water to stop the cooking, drain again really well, and transfer to a bowl to cool.
Pour over the olive oil, mix in the tomatoes and capers, and season. Scatter over the gremolata and serve.

Advance preparation: Chop the tomatoes, cook the pasta, zest the lemons, and chop the garlic up to 4 hours before; cover and chill. Assemble up to 1 hour before serving.
Freezing: Not suitable.

Asian ravioli with soy-butter sauce

Instead of making my own ravioli dough, I use wonton skins. SERVES 10

5 sprigs parsley or cilantro
Vegetable oil for deep-frying
60 wonton wrappers
1 tblsp cornstarch
2 recipes Shiitake Mushroom & Ginger
  Filling (page 40)
for the soy-butter sauce
⅞ cup red wine vinegar
⅓ cup beef stock
⅓ cup light soy sauce
1¾ cups (3½ sticks) unsalted butter
¼ cup lemon juice
Salt & freshly ground pepper to taste

Heat some oil for deep-frying to 400°F. Deep-fry the parsley or cilantro for about 30 seconds, or until crisp, then drain well on paper towels.
Lay the wonton wrappers out on a surface lightly dusted with cornstarch. Brush the edges with water.
Divide the mushroom mixture between half the wrappers, placing it in the center. Cover these with a second wonton wrapper and press the edges together.
Make the sauce by vigorously boiling the vinegar, stock, and soy sauce together in a small saucepan until reduced by half.
Dice the butter and whisk it into the sauce over medium heat, a piece at a time, to make a creamy emulsion. Add the lemon juice and season to taste.

Penne with tomatoes & basil gremolata

Remove from the heat and keep the sauce hot by setting it over a pan of warm water.

Cook the ravioli in batches in a large pan of boiling salted water for 2 minutes or until light and plump. Remove with a slotted spoon.

Arrange the ravioli on a dish, drizzle over the soy-butter sauce, and garnish with the deep-fried parsley or cilantro. Serve.

Advance preparation: Fill the ravioli up to 4 hours before and put onto a tray dusted with cornstarch; cover and chill. Fry the parsley; make the sauce up to 1 hour before and keep warm. Cook the ravioli to order.
Freezing: Make and freeze the mushroom mixture up to 4 weeks ahead.

Bacon & egg linguine

A fantastic combination: the best of British coupled with the best of Italy. SERVES 10

10 oz pancetta or bacon
1½ lb dried linguine or spaghetti
10 large eggs
Olive oil for frying
⅔ cup extra-virgin olive oil
2½ cups (8 oz) grated Parmesan cheese
2 tblsp chopped fresh parsley
Salt & freshly ground pepper to taste

Fry the pancetta or bacon in a hot frying pan for 2–3 minutes or until very crisp. Drain on paper towels and crumble. Keep warm in a 325°F oven.

Cook the pasta in a large pan of boiling water for 7–10 minutes or until al dente.

Fry the eggs for 2–3 minutes in hot oil over medium heat, keeping the yolk runny. Keep warm at the side of the stove.

Drain the pasta, transfer to a dish, and pour over the extra-virgin olive oil. Add the Parmesan and lots of seasoning, and toss.

Divide among individual bowls. Put a fried egg on top of each, then some pancetta and parsley. Serve immediately.

Advance preparation: Cook the pancetta or bacon and chop the parsley 1 day before; cover and chill. Cook the pasta and eggs to order.
Freezing: Cook and freeze the pancetta or bacon 4 weeks ahead. Crisp in a preheated 375°F oven for 3–4 minutes.

Laksa noodle salad

Laksa is a glorious Singaporean broth, made from a spice paste and enriched with coconut milk before adding rice noodles, bean sprouts, and vegetables. Here, I use the laksa as a dressing and top the noodles with crisp raw vegetables. SERVES 10

2 tblsp vegetable oil

⅔ cup coconut milk

2 large carrots

1 lb wide rice noodles

1 cucumber

1 cup bean sprouts

A few mizuna or tat-soi leaves to garnish

for the laksa paste

1 small onion, chopped

1 large clove garlic, crushed

2 tsp finely grated fresh ginger

1 stalk lemongrass, white part only

2 tblsp macadamia nuts

½ tsp shrimp paste

1 tsp hot red chili flakes

½ tsp ground turmeric

½ tsp ground coriander

½ tsp ground cumin

Grind all the laksa paste ingredients together, either with a pestle and mortar or in a food processor, until smooth.

Fry the paste in oil over medium heat for 2–3 minutes. Lower the heat, pour in the coconut milk, and cook for 5 minutes or until the mixture is the consistency of thick pouring cream. Cool.

Cut the carrots and cucumber into paper-thin shavings with a vegetable peeler. Put the carrot shavings into a bowl of ice water and leave for 30 minutes so that they curl. Drain well on paper towels.

Put the noodles in a bowl, pour over boiling water, soak for 5 minutes, and then drain and pat dry carefully. Transfer to a serving dish.

Toss the noodles in the laksa paste, or alternatively, spoon it over the noodles. Strew the vegetables, bean sprouts, and mizuna or tat-soi over the top and serve.

Advance preparation: Make and fry the laksa paste with the coconut milk up to 4 days before; cover and chill. Prepare the carrots and put into water, and cut the cucumber up to 6 hours ahead; cover and chill. Assemble the salad up to 1 hour before; cover and chill.
Freezing: Not suitable.

Crispy noodle chicken salad

This Asian-style salad has lovely clean, fresh-tasting flavors, perfect for hot summer days. SERVES 10

for the salad

Vegetable oil for deep-frying

5 oz rice stick noodles

1 tblsp toasted sesame oil

8 oz fresh shiitake mushrooms

1 lb fresh or bottled baby corn

1 lb cooked chicken breast, thinly sliced

1 lb medium shrimp, cooked, shelled & deveined

2 cups bean sprouts

5 scallions, sliced diagonally

Salt to taste

for the dressing

6 tblsp fresh lime juice

¼ cup Thai fish sauce

¼ cup red wine vinegar

2 hot red chilies, seeded & thinly sliced

1 clove garlic, crushed

1 heaping tsp sugar

Heat some oil for deep-frying to 375°F. Deep-fry the rice sticks in batches for 30 seconds or until puffed up and lightly colored.

Transfer onto paper towels to drain, sprinkle liberally with salt while still hot, then let cool.

Heat a wok or sauté pan, pour in the sesame oil, and fry the mushrooms for 2 minutes over medium heat until cooked but firm. Drain on paper towels.

Cook the fresh corn in boiling water for 3 minutes or until just tender. Drain and refresh in cold water, then drain well on paper towels. Or, use bottled corn.

Mix all the ingredients together for the salad dressing.

Put the rice sticks in a serving dish. Toss the rest of the salad ingredients in the

Laksa noodle salad

dressing and arrange them in a separate dish. Serve.

Advance preparation: Cook the rice sticks, mushrooms, corn, chicken, and shrimp and make the dressing up to 1 day in advance. Store the noodles in an airtight container and everything else separately covered in the fridge. Assemble up to 2 hours before.
Freezing: Not suitable.

Buckwheat noodles with chestnuts & wild mushrooms

Vacuum-packed chestnuts are a godsend as they are so time-consuming to prepare otherwise. Their earthy, sweet nutty taste complements the wild mushrooms and noodles splendidly. SERVES 10

1 lb mixed wild mushrooms
⅔ cup (1⅓ sticks) butter
14 oz vacuum-packed chestnuts
2 large cloves garlic, crushed
3½ cups heavy cream
5 tblsp chopped fresh parsley
2 tblsp fresh lemon juice
12 oz buckwheat (soba) noodles
Salt & freshly ground pepper to taste

Sauté the mushrooms in batches in the butter over high heat for 3–4 minutes. Set aside. Sauté the chestnuts and garlic for 2 minutes in the same pan.

Return the mushrooms to the pan with the chestnuts and add the cream. Bring to a boil, lower the heat, and simmer for 2 minutes. Stir in the parsley, lemon juice, and seasoning .

Boil the noodles in a large pan of water for 4 minutes or until al dente. Drain, pour over the mushroom sauce, stir, and serve.

Advance preparation: Make the mushroom sauce up to 4 hours ahead; cover and chill. Reheat over low heat for 5–7 minutes, adding a little water if necessary. Cook the noodles to order. *Freezing: Not suitable.*

the menu

Vodka cherry tomatoes with herbed garlic salt

Sesame cheese straws

Parmesan toasts

Anchovy pastries

Curry puffs

Crispy noodle chicken salad

Asian coleslaw

Cucumber, sugar snap & radish salad

Mojitos

Watermelon frappé

Clockwise from top right:
Fruity frappés offer refreshment on hot days; Asian Coleslaw is an exotic twist on a traditional picnic favorite; pack food in disposable cartons for easy eating, and because you will not want to wash up after a fun day out; fresh chilies add bite to Crispy Noodle Chicken Salad; when everything is easy to carry and clear up you will resolve to have picnics more often.

picnic

124

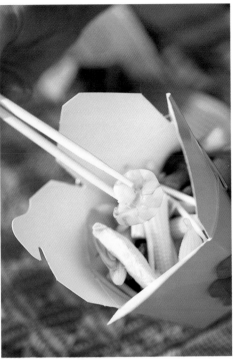

Clockwise from top right:
*Chopsticks make convenient
picnic utensils, and so do fingers
(here used to dip marinated
cherry tomatoes in herby salt);
Curry Puffs are quickly made
from bought pastry and your
favorite curry paste; take a box
of tasty crispy things to snack on
throughout the day; a fresh
salad of cucumber, sugar snaps,
and radishes complements the
noodle dish; Mojito, a good hot
weather drink, served in cups.*

Green salad

*The contents of a green salad are very much
a matter of personal preference and depend
on what you plan to serve it with. You
ideally want a mixture of something peppery
like arugula, mustard greens, or watercress;
something mild, which might be mâche or
baby spinach; and something bitter such as
Belgian endive or curly endive. Then, I like
to throw in a delicate leaf such as miner's
lettuce, which looks like a tiny lily pad with
a speck of a white flower. Herbs — chervil,
basil, cilantro, and so on — can also be
added, however do not overdo the choice of
leaves or you will have too many competing
flavors in the salad. Three, or four,
maximum, varieties will do. Always tear
leaves, never cut them, and wash and dry
them really well so as not to dilute the
dressing. Dressings, too, can be varied, but if
the salad is to accompany another dish, or
several dishes, I tend to use fruity olive oil·
and balsamic or wine vinegar.* SERVES 10

5 oz mixed salad greens
2 tblsp balsamic vinegar
¼ cup extra-virgin olive oil
Salt & freshly ground pepper to taste

Tear all the salad leaves to bite-sized
pieces.
Add salt and pepper to the vinegar, then
mix in the oil.
Toss the salad greens in the dressing and
serve immediately.

Advance preparation: Make the
dressing up to 2 days ahead; cover.
Wash, dry, but do not tear the salad up to
1 day before; cover and chill. Toss in the
dressing to order.
Freezing: Not suitable.

right Green mango & papaya salad

Tomato salad

*To make this bold, beautiful salad, choose
lots of different varieties of tomato: stripy
green, orange, big ones, little ones, shiny red,
and sunny yellow. You could even throw in a
few home-roasted tomatoes. Then all they
need is a perfectly simple olive oil dressing
and a few fresh herbs.* SERVES 10

2½ lb mixed tomatoes, such as beefsteak,
   cherry, heirloom & Roma (plum)
   varieties
⅓ cup extra virgin olive oil
1 tbslp balsamic vinegar
1 heaping tblsp basil, marjoram,
   or oregano leaves
Fine sea salt and freshly ground pepper
   to taste

Slice the large tomatoes, halve the
medium-sized tomatoes, and leave the
small tomatoes whole. Arrange them
all in a serving dish.
Mix the oil and balsamic vinegar together
with some salt and pepper. Drizzle the
dressing over the tomatoes and sprinkle
with the herbs. Serve.

Advance preparation: Make the
dressing up to 2 days before and prepare
and arrange the tomatoes up to 3 hours
ahead; cover and chill. Remove from the
fridge 1 hour before serving; dress, add
herbs, and cover 30 minutes before.
Freezing: Not suitable.

Cucumber, sugar snap &
radish salad

*To ring the changes, substitute toasted sesame
seeds for the peanuts.* SERVES 10

for the salad
8 oz sugar snap peas
2 cucumbers, peeled
5 radishes, cut into thin strips
3 tblsp unsalted peanuts,
   toasted & coarsely chopped
for the rice wine vinegar dressing
2 tblsp rice wine vinegar or white wine
   vinegar
1 heaping tsp salt
1 heaping tsp sugar

Cook the sugar snap peas in boiling water for 2–3 minutes or until crisp-tender.

Drain and refresh in cold water until cold to preserve the color. Dry on paper towels and split in half.

Cut the cucumbers lengthwise into quarters, cut away the seeds, and slice into chunky diagonal pieces.

Place in a serving dish. Add the rice vinegar, salt, and sugar and mix well. Let stand for 10 minutes to let the flavors marry, stirring once or twice.

Add the sugar snaps, radishes, and peanuts just before serving so the vinegar does not discolor the sugar snaps.

Advance preparation: Toast and chop the peanuts up to 2 days ahead; keep covered. Prepare the rest of the salad ingredients up to 8 hours ahead, cover, and keep chilled in separate containers. *Freezing: Not suitable*

Green mango & papaya salad

It is worth trying to track down palm sugar, which can be found in Asian food stores and is sold as a syrup. A staple of Southeast Asian cooking, it is made from the boiled sap of coconut and palmyrah palms and has a dark, deep sweetness that enhances salads like this one no end. Use it to accompany the Red Duck Curry (page 99). SERVES 10

1 lb green mangoes, peeled and pitted
1¾ lb green papayas, peeled and seeded
1 small coconut, shelled
⅓ cup cilantro leaves
⅓ cup mint leaves
⅓ cup Thai basil leaves
for the dressing
2 tblsp palm sugar or dark brown sugar
1 tblsp boiling water
6 tblsp fresh lime juice
1 tblsp Thai fish sauce
Salt & freshly ground pepper to taste

Mix all the dressing ingredients together, stirring until the sugar dissolves.

Finely shred the mango and papaya into thin matchsticks.

Remove a third of the coconut and use a vegetable peeler to cut it into shavings for decoration. Shave the remainder and then shred it into thin matchsticks.

Toss the fruits, coconut matchsticks, and herbs together in the dressing. Arrange in a dish, scatter over the reserved coconut shavings, and serve.

Advance preparation: Make the dressing up to 2 days ahead; cover and chill. Shred the mango, papaya, and coconut up to 4 hours before; cover and chill. Assemble the salad up to 30 minutes before; cover and chill. *Freezing: Not suitable.*

Asian coleslaw

This crisp, pretty coleslaw with its light citrus-soy dressing is very quick and simple to make. SERVES 10

for the coleslaw
10 oz red cabbage
14 oz Napa cabbage
14 oz fennel
for the Asian dressing
6 tblsp orange juice
¼ cup rice wine vinegar
2 tblsp light soy sauce
4 tsp finely grated fresh ginger

Finely shred the cabbages and fennel.

Mix all the ingredients together for the dressing and pour over the coleslaw just 15 minutes before serving to prevent the salad from wilting.

Transfer to a salad bowl and serve.

Advance preparation: Make the dressing up to 2 days ahead; cover and chill. Prepare the vegetables up to 3 hours before and keep covered in the fridge. *Freezing: Not suitable.*

Arugula, French bean, red onion & crôuton salad

Serve this substantial salad on its own, or with a plate of cold cuts, for lunch or supper. SERVES 10

5 small red onions, quartered through
  the root
¾ cup olive oil
2 tblsp red wine vinegar
10 oz rustic bread, such as
  ciabatta, pugliese, or sourdough
5 oz French beans or baby Blue Lake
  green beans
3 cups arugula leaves
½ cup mixed olives, such as
  niçoise, kalamata & green
2½ tblsp capers, drained
for the garlic dressing
Salt & freshly ground pepper to taste
1½ tblsp red wine vinegar
1 clove garlic, crushed
4½ tblsp olive oil

Make the dressing by adding salt and
pepper into the vinegar. Add the garlic
and then the oil. Mix and let stand for
30 minutes to infuse.

Preheat the oven to 375°F. Put the
onions on a baking sheet and drizzle
them with 2 tablespoons of the olive oil
and the red wine vinegar. Cook for 25
minutes or until soft and tender.

Cut the bread, including the crust, into
1-inch cubes. Put them onto a baking
sheet, moisten with the rest of the olive
oil, and bake for 10–15 minutes or until
golden, shaking them occasionally. Drain
on paper towels and season with salt.

Cook the beans in boiling salted water for
3–4 minutes or until crisp-tender. Drain,
then refresh in cold water until cold. Dry
the beans on paper towels and cut in half
diagonally.

Put all the salad ingredients in a bowl,
add the dressing, and toss well. Serve.

left Arugula, haricots verts, red onion & crôuton
salad

Advance preparation: Make the croûtons up to 4 days before and cover. Warm them in a preheated 350°F oven for 5 minutes to freshen. Make the dressing up to 2 days ahead. Roast the onions, cook the beans, wash and dry the arugula up to 1 day before; cover and chill. Toss the salad to order.
Freezing: Make and freeze the croûtons up to 4 weeks ahead. Crisp as above.

Potato, watercress & walnut salad

The Chicken Tonnato (page 96) and Roast Beef Salad (page 95) would be splendid main courses to serve with this peppery watercress and potato salad. SERVES 10

1 lb small waxy potatoes
12 oz watercress
1 cup (4 oz) walnuts
Salt & freshly ground pepper to taste
for the walnut oil dressing
3 tblsp red wine or cider vinegar
2 tsp Dijon mustard
Salt to taste
¼ cup walnut oil

Make the dressing by mixing the vinegar and mustard together in a small bowl with some salt. Stir in the oil.
Cook the potatoes in boiling salted water for 10–12 minutes or until tender. Drain, cool a little, cut in half, and then pour over half the dressing and mix well. The potatoes will absorb more flavor if you do this while they are still hot. Season.
Toss the warm or cold potatoes, watercress, and walnuts together in the remaining dressing and serve.

Advance preparation: Make the dressing up to 2 days before and cook and dress the potatoes (if serving cold) up to 1 day ahead; cover and chill. Toss the salad to order.
Freezing: Not suitable.

Mozzarella with olives, anchovies & parsley

Mozzarella with olives, anchovies & parsley

I always think mozzarella needs a helping hand and should be teamed with distinctively flavored ingredients. The Olive & Parsley salad is ideal for this purpose. This dish is a good accompaniment to some sliced prosciutto di Parma and can be served as a first course or lunch dish. SERVES 10

2 recipes coarsely chopped Olive & Parsley Salad, made without lemon zest (page 42)
⅓ cup sun-dried tomatoes in oil, drained and coarsely chopped
2 tblsp coarsely chopped anchovies
4 balls mozzarella, each cut into 5 pieces
2 tblsp olive oil

Make the olive & parsley salad the same way as on page 42, but chop everything much less finely. Add the sun-dried tomatoes and anchovies and mix well.
Arrange the mozzarella on a platter, spoon over the olive-parsley mixture, and drizzle with the oil. Serve.

Advance preparation: Refer to the Olive-Parsley Salad recipe. Chop the sun-dried tomatoes and anchovies and store separately, covered, in the fridge up to 1 day before. Combine the olive-parsley salad up to 4 hours ahead and assemble with the cheese up to 30 minutes before; cover and chill.
Freezing: Not suitable.

Roasted vegetables

Everyone adores roasted vegetables and this dish is no exception. The vegetables are sweet, sticky, and crisp all at the same time. Try them with the Chicken Scaloppine (page 97), omitting the roasted red and yellow cherry tomatoes in that recipe, or serve them as a simple main-course supper dish in their own right with good bread. SERVES 10

5 Roma (plum) tomatoes, halved
  lengthwise
¾ cup olive oil
A large pinch of sugar
1½ lb sweet potatoes, cut into chunks
1½ lb parsnips, cut into chunks
1 lb shallots (halved lengthwise if large)
12 oz small brown mushrooms
2 tsp chopped fresh thyme leaves
Salt & freshly ground pepper to taste

Preheat the oven to 375°F. Put the tomatoes skin side down in a roasting pan, drizzle with 2 tablespoons of the olive oil, and sprinkle with the sugar, plus some salt and pepper.

Roast the tomatoes for 30 minutes or until soft and slightly charred. Remove them from the pan while warm, place on paper towels and set aside.

Raise the temperature of the oven to 400°F. Divide the sweet potato, parsnips, and shallots between 2 roasting pans and toss the vegetables in ½ cup of the olive oil.

Roast them for 45–60 minutes, turning and basting the vegetables halfway through cooking and switching the pans between the shelves at the same time.

Toss the mushrooms and thyme in the remaining oil. Add them and the roasted tomatoes to the other vegetables and roast

15 minutes longer or until everything is tender and golden.

Drain all the vegetables on paper towels, then season to taste and serve.

Advance preparation: Roast, cool and chill the tomatoes 2 days before. Cook the sweet potatoes, parsnips, and shallots 4 hours before. Reheat them to order at 400°F for 20 minutes, adding the mushrooms, thyme, and roast tomatoes to the pans 5 minutes later.
Freezing: Not suitable.

Stir-fried bok choy, asparagus & sugar snaps

You could add, or substitute, shiitake mushrooms, baby corn, Napa cabbage, or bean sprouts to those vegetables I've suggested here. The Red Duck Curry (page 99) and Asian Ravioli (page 118) would benefit from being served with this quick dish. SERVES 10

1 lb baby bok choy, halved lengthwise
1 lb asparagus, halved diagonally
8 oz scallions, halved lengthwise
8 oz sugar snap peas
One 2-inch piece fresh ginger, cut
  into fine strips
2 cloves garlic, crushed
2 tblsp toasted sesame oil
2 tblsp Thai fish sauce
1 tsp palm sugar or dark brown sugar

Toss all the vegetables together with the ginger and garlic.

Heat the oil in a wok or large frying pan over high heat. Add the vegetables and stir-fry for 2–3 minutes, constantly moving the vegetables around the pan.

Add the fish sauce and sugar, stir some more, and cook for another 30 seconds or until crisp-tender. Serve immediately.

Advance preparation: Prepare all the vegetables, ginger, and garlic up to 8 hours ahead and keep separate, covered, in the fridge. Stir-fry to order.
Freezing: Not suitable.

Roasted vegetables

Scarlet & green beans

If you omit the butter, you can serve these beans cold as a salad, tossed in a trickle of extra-virgin olive oil and balsamic vinegar. Scour the shops for different types of beans and use whatever is best that day. SERVES 10

1½ lb scarlet runner or cranberry beans, shelled

12 oz green beans

12 oz yellow green beans, Romano beans, or lima beans, shelled

12 oz French beans or baby Blue Lake green beans

1¼ lb fava beans, shelled

4 tblsp butter, melted

Salt & freshly ground pepper to taste

Put the scarlet runner beans in a pan of cold unsalted water and bring to a boil. Lower the heat, cover, and simmer for 8–10 minutes or until tender.

Remove the beans with a slotted spoon, drain, and dry on paper towels.

Use the same large pan of boiling salted water to cook the rest of the beans until they are tender but still have some bite. Top up with more boiling water during cooking if necessary. Cook the beans in the following order and for the following amount of time: green, romano, or lima beans, 4–6 minutes; French beans or Blue Lakes, 3–4 minutes; fava beans 2–3 minutes.

Drain all the beans in a colander under cold running water to preserve the color. Dry on paper towels.

Preheat the oven to 375°F. Peel the fava beans, discarding the skins.

Toss all the cooked beans in the melted butter, season, and put into an ovenproof serving dish. Cover and heat in the oven for 12–15 minutes or until hot. Serve.

Advance preparation: Cook all the beans up to 1 day ahead, cover, and chill. Toss in the butter and season up to 4 hours before; cover. Heat as above.
Freezing: Not suitable.

right Stir-fried bok choy, asparagus & sugar snaps

Red berry kissel with biscotti & vanilla cream

I have made this kissel for years now and never tire of it. It is a luscious compote of soft red fruits, and I use it in lots of different ways. Try it on hot waffles with a scoop of ice cream, spooned onto sweet bruschetta bread, or on hot cinnamon toast with lashings of crème fraîche. I've also had great success when I've used it as a filling for summer puddings and as a topping for a tart filled with sweetened mascarpone. When brides want to serve their chocolate Sachertorte wedding cake (page 141) as a dessert, this kissel accompanies it exquisitely. In winter, any frozen berries (apart from strawberries) work successfully. Serve the kissel with something crisp like biscotti or a deep-fried wonton wrapper dusted with cinnamon and sugar (page 78). SERVES 10

20 biscotti
for the kissel
3 cups raspberries
¼ cup water
½ cup sugar + extra
  to taste
⅔ cup fresh orange juice
2½ cups dry red wine
1 heaping tblsp cornstarch
12 cups mixed soft berries, such as
  blackberries, pitted cherries, currants,
  raspberries & strawberries
for the vanilla cream
1 vanilla bean, halved lengthwise
1¼ cups heavy cream
1 tblsp superfine sugar

Put the raspberries, water, and sugar for the kissel in a pan and cook over low heat for 3–4 minutes or until the raspberries just begin to soften. Remove from the heat, purée in a blender or processor and then sieve to remove the seeds.
Put the raspberry purée, orange juice, and wine in a saucepan and bring to a boil.
Take 3 tablespoons of the hot liquid and mix it with the cornstarch. Add this mixture to the pan, bring to a boil, and stir well for 2 minutes or until thickened. Cool the sauce until it is barely warm.
Remove the seeds from the vanilla bean with a teaspoon and add them to the cream with the sugar.
Beat the cream until soft peaks form, then spoon it into a bowl.
Fold all the prepared fruits, except any strawberries, into the warm sauce and add sugar to taste. Leave to cool and add any strawberries when the sauce is cold. The sauce should lightly coat the fruits. Serve with the cream and biscotti.

Advance preparation: Make the kissel, without adding the strawberries, up to 2 days before; cover and chill. Add the strawberries to the kissel and whisk the cream up to 4 hours before; cover and chill. Stir both lightly before serving. *Freezing: Freeze the kissel, without strawberries, up to 4 weeks ahead.*

Baked peaches with figs, ginger & spices

An autumnal dish of baked peaches (you could also use apples), stuffed with dried fruits and nuts and spiced up with stem ginger, nutmeg, and cardamom. Serve with some yogurt cheese. SERVES 10

⅓ cup hazelnuts
3 tblsp unsalted butter
8 oz dried figs, sliced
⅓ cup stem ginger in syrup,
  drained and sliced
½ tsp grated nutmeg
½ tsp ground cardamom
Grated zest & juice of 2 oranges
⅓ cup muscat or sweet white wine
10 peaches

Preheat the oven to 375°F. Roast the hazelnuts for 5 minutes and then halve them. Leave the oven on.
Mix together the nuts, butter, figs, ginger, spices, orange zest, juice, and wine.
Cut a 1½-inch circle around the top of the peaches and then push the knife down to cut around the pit. Twist the pit out, being careful not to damage the flesh of the fruit.
Put the peaches, side by side, in an ovenproof serving dish. Fill the center of the fruit with the stuffing and pour over

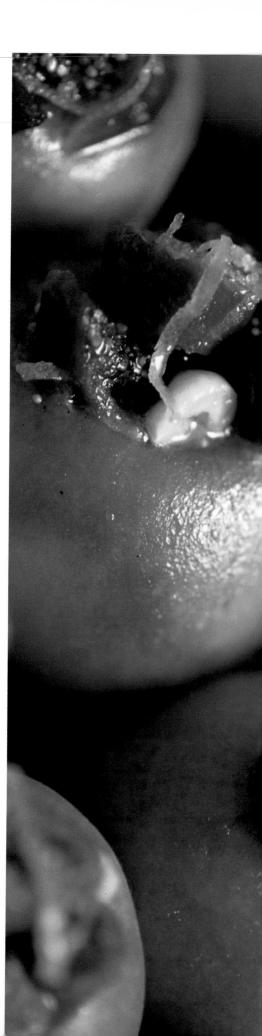

any remaining juices. Bake the peaches for 20–25 minutes or until soft, then serve.

Advance preparation: Make the stuffing up to 3 days ahead; cover and chill. Stuff the peaches up to 4 hours before and bake to order.
Freezing: Make and freeze the stuffing up to 4 weeks before.

Rolled pavlova with mango & passion fruit

This is the most divine, melt-in-the-mouth dessert: pure white, soft meringue filled with cream and tropical fruits. Try it in summer months marbled with cream, lemon curd, and lots of ripe red berries. SERVES 10

for the pavlova
6 large egg whites
¾ cup superfine sugar
½ cup confectioners' sugar + 1 tblsp extra for dusting
1 tblsp cornstarch

for the mango & passion fruit sauce
1 large mango, peeled and cut from pit
4 passion fruit, seeded and juiced
2 tblsp fresh lime juice
1–2 tblsp sugar

for the filling
2 passion fruit, seeded and juiced
1¼ cups heavy cream
1 large mango, peeled, cut from pit, and thinly sliced

for the decoration
⅔ cup heavy cream, lightly whipped
You will also need a baking sheet approximately 10 x 15 inches, some parchment paper, a pastry bag, and a ½-inch star pastry tip

Preheat the oven to 375°F and line the baking sheet with parchment paper.
Beat the egg whites until they are stiff but not dry.
Sieve together the sugars and cornstarch for the pavlova. Beat them into the egg whites, 1 tablespoon at a time, until the meringue is thick.

Spread the meringue onto the baking sheet and smooth the top with a spatula. Bake for 8 minutes or until light golden, firm, and slightly rubbery to touch. Transfer the meringue to a wire rack to cool.
Purée the meringue onto a piece of parchment paper lightly dusted with confectioners' sugar, then peel off the paper on which the meringue was baked.
Blend the mango for the sauce in a blender or processor until smooth and then sieve. To make the sauce, mix together the mango purée, passion fruit seeds and juice, and lime juice, and add sugar to taste. Set aside until ready to serve.
Beat lightly the cream for the filling, then fold in the passion fruit seeds and juice. Spread this mixture onto the cooled meringue.
Arrange the sliced mango on top of the cream, reserving 10 slices to decorate.
Roll up the filled pavlova carefully, pushing it away from you and using the parchment to help you do so.
Dust the pavlova with confectioners' sugar and carefully lift it onto a serving dish.
Whip lightly the cream for the decoration. Pipe rosettes of the cream onto the pavlova and decorate with the reserved slices of mango. Serve with the passion fruit sauce.

Advance preparation: Bake the meringue and make the sauce up to 1 day before; chill the meringue, uncovered, and chill the sauce, covered. Assemble the pavlova up to 4 hours before, undecorated; cover and chill. Decorate 1 hour before serving.
Freezing: The sauce can be made and frozen up to 4 weeks ahead.

left Baked peaches with figs, ginger & spices

Increase the heat a little, without letting the mixture boil, and whisk until frothy. Set aside and keep warm.

Add the orange oil and zest to the choux pastry dough, mix well, and transfer the dough to a piping bag with nozzle.

Heat the oil to 350°F. Pipe the choux pastry into the oil in 4-inch loops, 3 at a time. Turn them once and cook for 1–1½ minutes or until crisp and golden.

Drain the churros on paper towels and dredge well confectioners' sugar.

Pour the hot chocolate into glasses and serve immediately with the churros to dip.

Advance preparation: Make the flavored choux pastry, cover, and chill; make, cool, cover, and chill the hot chocolate up to 1 day before. Heat the hot chocolate over low heat for 10 minutes and fry the churros to order. *Freezing: Make and freeze the flavored choux pastry up to 4 weeks ahead.*

Apple & blackberry filo pastries

Filo pastry is such an asset for making desserts in a hurry. Here, it is topped with wafer-thin slices of apple and strewn with a few ripe blackberries. Keep the filo covered with a clean damp cloth while making this dish to keep it from drying out. SERVES 10

16 sheets filo pastry, measuring about 17½ x 7inches
½ cup (1 stick) unsalted butter, melted, + extra for greasing
5 Granny Smith or other tart apples, peeled & very finely sliced
2 cups blackberries
3 tblsp superfine sugar
1 tblsp confectioners' sugar
1¼ cups heavy cream, lightly whipped

Brush 1 sheet of pastry with some of the melted butter. Put another sheet on top and brush this lightly with butter too. Continue until you have a total of 8 layers.
Repeat with the remaining pastry and butter to make another stack. Cut each stack into 5 rectangles measuring about 3½ x 7 inches.

Orange churros with hot chocolate

Orange churros with hot chocolate

Now, neither the churros nor the hot chocolate actually need each other, as both are wonderful in their own right. But the combination of the two is a knockout and just right for serving at brunches when everyone needs something hot and sweet to give their Sunday a kick-start (they are also good for tea or to end a meal). Churros, or Spanish breakfast fritters, are often dipped into a cup of coffee. In Spain they make them with a flour and water batter, but mine are made from choux pastry flavored with orange oil. Specialty foods shops sell this orange oil in small bottles. If you can't find it, add extra orange zest to compensate. SERVES 10

for the hot chocolate
1 lb semisweet chocolate
6 cups milk
for the orange churros
2 recipes Choux Pastry dough (page 81)
1 tsp orange oil
1 tsp grated orange zest
Vegetable oil for deep-frying
2 tblsp confectioners' sugar
You will also need a pastry bag and ½-inch star pastry tip

Break the chocolate into squares and place them in a pan with the milk. Heat them gently over low heat or about 10 minutes or until the chocolate has completely melted.

Arrange the apple in overlapping layers on top of the pastries and divide the blackberries among them. Brush the pastries all over with the remaining butter and sprinkle them with superfine sugar.

Preheat the oven to 350°F. Put the pastries onto 2 lightly greased baking sheets and bake them for 20 minutes or until golden, switching the trays in the oven halfway through cooking.

Dust the pastries with confectioners' sugar and serve them with the whipped cream.

Advance preparation: Bake the pastries up to 4 hours before and cover. Reheat in a preheated 350°F oven at for 5–7 minutes.
Freezing: Not suitable.

Apricot tart

This is a lovely classic French tart. Other stone fruits such as plums and peaches are good used instead of apricots. SERVES 10

⅓ recipe Sweet Pastry (page 80)
Flour for dusting
for the filling
3 tblsp ground almonds
20 apricots, halved & pitted
⅔ cup heavy cream
2 large eggs, lightly beaten
⅓ cup vanilla sugar
1½ tsp vanilla extract
2 tblsp confectioners' sugar
You will also need a 9-inch or 10-inch square or round false-bottomed, shallow fluted tart pan, some parchment paper, and dried beans or pie weights

Roll the chilled pastry out thinly on a lightly floured surface until it is 2 inches larger than the pan.

Wrap the pastry around the rolling pin and let it unroll over the pan, pressing it down into the bottom and up the sides. Roll the pin over the top of the pan to trim away any excess pastry.

Prick the base of the pastry shell with a fork and chill for 30 minutes.

Preheat the oven to 375°F. Line the tart with parchment paper and dried beans or pie weights and bake for 15 minutes or until golden. Remove the parchment and beans or weights and bake 5 minutes longer.

Remove the pastry shell from the oven and set aside to cool slightly. Lower the oven temperature to 350°F.

Sprinkle the almonds on the bottom of the pastry shell and arrange the apricots on top, cut side up.

Whisk together the cream, eggs, vanilla sugar, and extract. Pour this mixture into the pastry shell and bake for 45–50 minutes, or until the custard has set and the apricots are slightly caramelized.

Cool for 10 minutes before removing the tart from the pan to a serving dish. Dust with confectioners' sugar and serve hot or cold.

Advance preparation: Bake the pastry shell and mix the custard up to 1 day before; store the tart in an airtight container; cover and chill the custard. Bake to order if serving hot, allowing an extra 5 minutes' cooking time. If serving cold, bake up to 12 hours ahead; cover and chill. Remove from the fridge 1 hour before serving.
Freezing: The tart case can be frozen unbaked in its pan for up to 1 week and baked straight from the freezer. Freeze it baked up to 3 weeks ahead.

Apple & blackberry filo pastries

Raspberry & lemon syllabub trifle

Trifle, but not as we know it: Day-Glo jelly, lumpy custard, rubbery sponge cake, canned fruits, and, of course, the inevitable decoration of maraschino cherries. My trifle is a far cry from that: a sensuous stack of buttery brioches, billowing lemon syllabub, vanilla cream, and fresh raspberries.
SERVES 10

5 individual brioches, each cut into 4 pieces
¼ cup sweet white wine or sherry
1¼ cups raspberries
2 recipes Lemon Syllabub (page 81)
1 tblsp confectioners' sugar
3 tblsp candied citrus peel, cut into
   thin shavings

for the raspberry sauce
⅔ cup raspberries
1 tblsp water
2 tblsp granulated sugar

for the vanilla cream
1 vanilla bean, halved lengthwise
⅔ cup heavy cream
2 tsp granulated sugar

Make the sauce by heating the raspberries, water, and sugar in a saucepan over low heat for 3–4 minutes or until the raspberries just begin to soften. **Remove** from the heat and cool. Purée in a blender or processor, then sieve.

Scrape the seeds from the vanilla bean and add them to the cream with the sugar. Beat until soft peaks form.

Place a slice of brioche on a dessert plate. Drizzle it with some wine, spoon on some vanilla cream, then a few raspberries and a spoonful of raspberry purée. Top it with another slice of brioche, some more wine and then some syllabub.

Decorate by arranging a few pieces of citrus peel on top and lightly dusting the whole thing with confectioners' sugar. Repeat with the remaining ingredients and serve.

Advance preparation: Make the fruit sauce and syllabub up to 1 day before; cover and chill. Whisk the syllabub a little if it separates. Assemble up to 1½ hours before; cover and chill. Remove from the fridge 30 minutes before eating.
Freezing: Make and freeze the raspberry sauce up to 4 weeks in advance.

Saffron cream with sesame–poppy seed wafers

Saffron cream with sesame–poppy seed wafers

This saffron cream is the simplest dessert in the world to make, and apart from allowing time for the saffron to infuse, it truly takes just 5 minutes from start to finish. The wafers take a bit longer. They have a real nutty crunch to them, which a dessert as rich as this needs. SERVES 10

for the sesame–poppy seed wafers
2 tblsp unsalted butter +
  extra for greasing
¼ cup turbinado sugar
2 tblsp honey
2 tblsp poppy seeds
2½ tblsp sesame seeds
for the saffron cream
3 tblsp warm milk
18–20 saffron threads
3 cups crème fraîche
⅓ cup granulated sugar

Put the butter, sugar, and honey in a saucepan and bring to a boil. Add the sesame and poppy seeds, stir well, and set aside to cool completely.

Preheat the oven to 400°F. Divide the mixture into 20 small balls. Place them well apart on lightly greased baking sheets and flatten with your thumb.

Bake for about 5 minutes or until slightly darker in color. Transfer the wafers to a wire rack to cool and harden.

Mix the milk and saffron threads together and let infuse for 10 minutes.

Place the crème fraîche and sugar in a bowl and pour in the saffron milk. Beat with an electric mixer at high speed for 1½ minutes or until light and aerated.

Spoon the saffron cream into a dish and serve with 2 wafers per person.

Advance preparation: Make the saffron cream 4 days before; cover and chill. Stir before serving. Make the wafers 3 days before and store in an airtight container.
Freezing: Make and freeze the wafers up to 4 weeks ahead, layered between sheets of parchment paper. Crisp, if needed, in a preheated 400°F oven for 2 minutes. Cool before serving.

Chocolate mousse with espresso granita & stenciled cookies

Chocolate, coffee, and more chocolate. This is a very decadent pudding of dark chocolate mousse, rich heavy cream, and bitter espresso coffee granita. And then, just to gild the lily, there are some frivolous stenciled chocolate cookies to go with it. SERVES 10

1¼ cups heavy cream, lightly whipped
for the espresso granita
¼ cup granulated sugar
⅔ cup boiling water
⅔ cup very strong espresso coffee
for the stenciled cookies
½ recipe Chocolate Cookie Dough (page 84)
Flour for dusting
2 tblsp confectioners' sugar
for the chocolate mousse
12 oz semisweet chocolate, chopped

⅓ cup very strong espresso coffee
1 tblsp orange liqueur, such as Cointreau or Grand Marnier
1 tblsp unsalted butter
3 large egg yolks, separated
1 large egg white
You will also need a 2¾-inch round cutter, some parchment paper, an X-acto blade and an ice cream scoop

Make the granita by dissolving the sugar in the boiling water, then stirring in the coffee. Cool and pour into a shallow metal tray. Freeze for 1 hour.

Break up the ice crystals with a fork, mixing them into any unfrozen coffee. Repeat every hour for 3 hours. Fork through the granita to make loose crystals.

Roll the chocolate cookie dough out to a thickness of ¼ inch on a lightly floured surface. Cut out 20 circles using the cutter and transfer to baking sheets. Chill for 30 minutes.

Melt the chocolate for the mousse in a large bowl over a pan of simmering water for about 10 minutes. Cool, add the coffee and liqueur, then beat in the butter and the egg yolks, one at a time.

Beat the egg whites until stiff but not dry and fold them into the chocolate mousse. Pour the mousse into a 2½- to 3-cup bowl, then cover and chill.

Preheat the oven to 350°F and bake the cookies for 8 minutes or until slightly darker in color. Transfer them to a wire rack to cool.

Make a stencil out of some parchment paper by cutting a 4-inch square and then marking a 2¾-inch circle in pen on this square. Draw ½-inch circles all over this circle, starting from the middle and leaving space in between. Carefully cut these small circles out using an X-acto blade.

Use the same method to make a striped stencil by drawing lines along the paper and cutting out every second strip.

Put the confectioners' sugar into a fine sieve, lay a stencil over a cookie, and lightly dust with the confectioners' sugar. Carefully remove the stencil and repeat with half the remaining cookies. Use the other stencil to decorate the last batch of cookies.

Scoop up some chocolate mousse and place in the bottom of an individual glass serving bowl. Cover the mousse with a dollop of whipped cream and finish with a spoonful of granita.

Repeat with the remaining ingredients and serve immediately with the cookies.

Advance preparation: Make the chocolate mousse 3 days before; cover and chill. Bake the cookies 2 days before and store in an airtight container; decorate 4 hours before and store uncovered.
Freezing: Freeze the cookies 3 weeks before; crisp in a preheated 350°F oven for 3–4 minutes. Make the granita 3 days before.

Chocolate mousse with espresso granita & stenciled cookies

Lime & pistachio kulfi with pistachio wafers

Lime & pistachio kulfi with pistachio wafers

Kulfi, much loved in India, is unlike other ice creams in that it needs no churning whatsoever. It's just a matter of mixing everything together and putting it in the freezer. I like to serve kulfi with translucent pistachio wafers. For an exotic, authentic touch, decorate each ice cream with a sheet of edible silver leaf, available from art stores.
SERVES 10

for the lime & pistachio kulfi
1 cup unsalted, peeled pistachio
   nuts, skinned
1 tblsp finely grated lime zest
6 tblsp superfine sugar
1 cup fresh lime juice
2½ cups canned evaporated milk
1 cup milk
A few drops of green food coloring
10 sheets silver leaf

for the pistachio wafers
Butter for greasing
3 egg whites
½ cup superfine sugar
⅔ cup all-purpose flour, sifted
⅓ cup unshelled unsalted pistachio nuts
You will also need ten 4-oz plastic kulfi molds or ramekins, a 1-lb loaf pan, parchment paper and 10 squares of banana leaf

Chop the pistachios for the kulfi in a blender or processor until they are very finely chopped but not a paste.
Add the rest of the ice cream ingredients, except the silver leaf, and process for 1 minute or until fairly smooth. Divide the mixture among the molds, cover, and freeze for 5 hours or until frozen.
Grease the loaf pan lightly and line it with parchment paper. Preheat the oven to 350°F.
Beat the egg whites for the wafers with an electric mixer until stiff, then beat in the sugar 1 tblsp at a time.
Fold the flour and nuts into the meringue to make a soft, spongelike mixture. Spoon into the loaf pan and smooth the top over. Bake for 40 minutes or until firm and golden.
Turn the loaf out on to a wire rack to cool and remove the paper. Reduce the oven temperature to 275°F.
Slice the cooled loaf as thinly as possible with a sharp, fine-bladed knife and lay the slices on baking sheets.
Bake the wafers for 6 minutes or until barely colored. Transfer them to a wire rack to cool and crisp.
Dip the ice cream molds in very hot water for 5 seconds. Run a small knife around the edges and turn the kulfi onto plates lined with squares of banana leaf.
Lift the silver leaf off its paper with the tip of a knife and use it to decorate the kulfi. Serve with the pistachio wafers.

Advance preparation: Make the wafers 1 week before and store in an airtight container layered with parchment paper. *Freezing: Freeze the kulfi 1 week ahead.*

Gilded Sachertorte

The only chocolate cake I ever make is this one, which has good keeping qualities and freezes very well. I vary it by changing the decoration. Often, it's simply festooned with fresh flowers. Other decorating ideas follow this basic recipe. SERVES 20

for the chocolate Sachertorte

3 large eggs, whole + 12 large eggs, separated

2½ cups sugar

1 lb semisweet chocolate, chopped

4 cups ground almonds

1 tblsp freshly ground coffee

for the icing

1 lb semisweet chocolate, chopped

¾ cup (1½ sticks) unsalted butter, cubed + extra for greasing

¼ cup smooth apricot jam

for the gilded decoration

12 sheets 23.5- to 24-carat transfer gold leaf

12 cape gooseberries, papery skins peeled back, or raspberries

You will also need a 10-inch round cake pan, some parchment paper, newspaper, and string

Line the base and insides of the greased pan with parchment paper. Wrap 4 layers of newspaper around the outside of the pan and tie with string. Preheat the oven to 375°F.

Beat the whole eggs, egg yolks, and sugar with an electric mixer for 10 minutes.

Melt the chocolate for the cake in a bowl over a pan of hot water. Stir it into the egg mixture with the almonds and coffee.

Beat the egg whites until stiff and carefully fold into the egg mixture.

Pour the mixture into the cake pan and cover the top of the cake with damp parchment paper. Bake for 1½ hours, dampening the parchment paper every 20 minutes. The cake is cooked when a skewer inserted in the center comes out clean.

Cool the cake in the cake pan for 1 hour before turning it out onto a wire rack.

Melt the chocolate for the icing in a bowl over a pan of hot water. Add the butter, bit by bit, stirring well. Cool the icing until it sets to a thick pouring consistency.

Trim the top of the cake, if necessary,

and turn it upside down on the wire rack.

Melt the jam in a small pan over a low heat, then brush it over the cake.

Pour the icing over the cake and smooth it evenly over the top and sides. Let the icing set for 2 hours before decorating.

Lay a sheet of gold leaf with its backing paper still on in the center of the cake. Use the back of a small round-bladed knife to gently rub the paper, transferring the gold onto the cake.

Remove the paper and continue to work your way around the cake with the rest of the gold leaf until the top is covered.

Arrange the cape gooseberries or raspberries on top of the gilded cake and serve.

Advance preparation: Bake the cake 1 week ahead, wrap well in 2 layers of foil, and store in an airtight container in a cool place. Ice up to 2 days ahead and store uncovered in the fridge (the condensation will disappear 4 hours after taking it out). Decorate 8 hours before and keep cool.
Freezing: Freeze the cake, wrapped as above, in an airtight container, 2 months before.

40-something cake

If piping messages onto cakes isn't your forte, use chocolate numbers or letters. SERVES 20

Chocolate Sachertorte + icing (left)

⅕ recipe Chocolate Cookie Dough (page 84)

Flour for rolling

2 tsp confectioners' sugar

2 tsp unsweetened cocoa powder

You will also need the appropriate 2-inch number cutters

Make and ice the cake as above, but do not gild or garnish.

Roll the dough out on a lightly floured surface until ¼-inch thick. Cut out 24 numbers using the cutters and transfer to baking sheets. Chill for 30 minutes.

Preheat the oven to 350°F and bake the cookies for 8 minutes. Transfer to a wire rack to cool.

Make small incisions in the cake with a sharp knife and poke the cookies into the incisions so that they stand up.

Dust the confectioners' sugar and cocoa

40-something cake

lightly over the top of the cake before serving.

Advance preparation: Decorate the cake up to 2 hours in advance and keep cool.
Freezing: Refer to basic recipe.

Heart cake with rose petals

This wedding cake can double as the dessert if served with some fresh berries, or kissel (page 132). You can also use this recipe to make 30 individual heart-shaped cakes about 3 inches wide. SERVES 50–60

1½ recipes Chocolate Sachertorte + icing (left)

10 large unsprayed roses, petals removed

You will also need a heart-shaped cake pan 12½ inches wide and 3½ inches deep

Make the cake as above, but bake for 2–2½ hours at 375°F. Ice, but do not gild or garnish.

Decorate by arranging the rose petals in a heart shape on top.

Advance preparation: Decorate 1–2 hours before serving and keep cool.
Freezing: Refer to basic recipe.

Left: *Use cinnamon sticks to stir steaming cups of Hot Buttered Rum — they add a festive element to the party and a delicious flavor to the drink.* Below: *Easy-to-make Roast Beef Salad is a rustic blend of Mediterranean pantry ingredients with a piquant creamy horseradish dressing.*

festive

Clockwise from top right:
Simple but stunning: Tomato Salad is made stylish with a variety of different shapes and colors, then dressed with balsamic vinaigrette, capers, and marjoram leaves; a pretty dusting of fine sugar gives this Apricot Tart, made from fresh fruit, a seasonal look; the secret of any successful buffet menu is not only in choosing dishes that taste delicious, they must also maintain their attractive appearance throughout the party and have guests coming back for second helpings.

the menu

Chicory with Roquefort, pecans & cranberries

Roast beef salad

Jambalaya

Tomato salad

Scarlet & green beans

Apricot tart

Chocolate martinis

Ginger cordial with star anise ice cubes

Hot buttered rum

Left: *Cubes of star anise set in ice make this ginger-flavored cocktail special. It contains no alcohol, ensuring that all guests feel welcome and cared for.*
Below: *An example of good menu planning: two hearty dishes, one hot, one cold, with differing textures, colors, and flavors. Guests can enjoy one, or both.*

Clockwise from above:
Scarlet & Green Beans can be served warm or cold; the classic martini is given a festive edge with a chocolate-rimmed glass and a curl of orange zest; traditional seasonal flavors of pecans, blue cheese, and cranberries combined in a canapé; shrimp jambalaya is hearty food for cold evenings, and easy to eat with a fork.

drinks

Guests want to eat, yes, but they also want to **drink and be merry**. Anyone can open a few bottles. Hosts with the most know the value of frivolity. **Kick-start** your party with a fun and funky **cocktail** — with or without alcohol. A fabulous frappé, a mesmerising mojito, a martini glass **rimmed with chocolate**. Fresh **fruits** are a focal point, whether embedded in ice cubes or creamed into a cooler. There's a small collection of **classics**, such as **Whisky Sours** and Negronis, for people who know what they like and want to stick with it. But we also **add sparkle** to old favorites, scooping **sorbet** into champagne, blending gold leaf into vodka, secreting an oyster in Clamato **juice**. You can run **hot and cold** in this chapter, with spicy warmers for indoors and out, for sipping by the bonfire, or bidding **farewell** to guests as they **venture** into the cold night air. And if you find anyone has not gone home, whip up the recipe for **Breakfast in a Glass**, remembering that **one mint julep** was not the cause of it all.

Sugar syrup

This syrup can be used for sweetening alcoholic and nonalcoholic drinks, or for adding to fruit sauces to serve with desserts. MAKES 2½ CUPS

2 cups water
2 cups sugar

Put the water in a pan, bring to a boil, add the sugar, and stir constantly for about 30 seconds or until the sugar has dissolved. To prevent the syrup from crystallizing, it is important that it completely dissolves. Reduce the heat to low.
Simmer the syrup for 5 minutes. Remove it from the heat and let it cool before using or storing in the fridge.

Advance preparation: Make up to 3 weeks ahead, cover, and chill.
Freezing: Not suitable.

Fruited ice cubes

Fruited ice cubes look beautiful floating in summery drinks, or even in a glass of sparkling mineral water. Citrus zest, edible flower petals such as borage and rose petals, and fresh cranberries for Christmas or Thanksgiving drinks can also be used instead of soft fruit.

Lemons or cucumber
A selection of soft fruit such as
  blackberries, cherries, raspberries,
  red currants & strawberries
Water
You will also need several ice-cube trays

Remove the zest from the lemons or peel from the cucumber in a thin coil using a paring knife or zester. Tie the strips into knots.
Divide the fruits and the knotted zest or peel among the ice-cube trays, fill with water, and freeze for 4–6 hours.
Remove the ice cubes from the trays and add to drinks just before serving.

Advance preparation: See below.
Freezing: Make the ice cubes up to 7 days in advance.

Lime, orange & lemon citrus pressés

If you want to decorate this refreshing drink with citrus zest knots, make them before you juice the fruit. Use a paring knife or zester to remove a thin coil of zest and then just twist this zest into a knot. MAKES 10

1¼ cups fresh lime juice
1¼ cups fresh orange juice
1¼ cups fresh lemon juice
1¼ cups sugar syrup
3½ cups sparkling mineral water
Ice cubes for serving

Mix all the ingredients together and serve poured over ice. Decorate with citrus zest knots, if desired.

Advance preparation: Make the knots and mix the juices up to 6 hours before; cover and chill. Add the water to order.
Freezing: Squeeze and freeze the juices up to 2 weeks ahead.

Ginger cordial with star anise ice cubes

Refreshing and aromatic, this is a good thirst quencher on hot days and accompanies Asian foods extremely well. SERVES 10

20 star anise pods
8 oz stem ginger in syrup
9 cups sparkling mineral water

Freeze the star anise with plain water in ice-cube trays for 4–6 hours.
Blend the ginger and all of its preserving syrup and a little of the mineral water in a blender or processor for about 1 minute or until puréed.
Divide the mixture among glasses, top up with the remaining water, and stir well.
Add the star anise ice cubes and serve.

Advance preparation: Purée the ginger, cover, and chill up to 7 days ahead. Dilute the ginger cordial to order.
Freezing: Make the ice cubes up to 7 days in advance.

Limey

This cooling summer drink can also be diluted with soda water instead of mineral water if you prefer. MAKES 10

1¼ cups fresh lime juice
1¼ cups fresh lemon juice
5 cups sparkling mineral water
Angostura or other bitters to taste
Ice cubes for serving

Mix the lime and lemon juice together.
Add the mineral water, stir, and add the bitters to taste. Serve over ice.

Advance preparation: Mix the juices up to 6 hours before, cover, and chill. Add the mineral water and bitters to order. *Freezing: Squeeze and freeze the lime and lemon juices up to 2 weeks before.*

Jasmine infusion

Scented edible flowers and herbs, such as jasmine, borage, elderflower, and variegated applemint can also be used to make this delicate infusion. Use sugar-encrusted swizzle sticks as decorative stirrers. MAKES 10

A handful of unsprayed jasmine flowers
   + a few extra for decoration
6 cups boiling water
10 sugar swizzle sticks

Put the jasmine flowers into a large French press and pour in the boiling water.
Leave them to infuse for 5 minutes before plunging the pot.
Pour the infusion into glasses, add a jasmine flower to each for decoration, and serve with the sugar swizzle sticks.

Advance preparation: Not suitable.
Freezing: Not suitable.

left Fruited ice cubes

Clear gazpacho

Serve small glasses of this clear tomato water, studded with tiny diced gazpacho vegetables, to greet your guests on a hot day, or to start a meal. Use really ripe tomatoes for the best results. MAKES 10

for the tomato water
4 lb beefsteak tomatoes, quartered
Freshly ground pepper to taste
2 tblsp salt
for the gazpacho vegetable garnish
1 beefsteak tomato
½ cucumber, finely diced
½ small yellow bell pepper, seeded
    and finely diced
½ medium avocado, peeled, pitted
    and finely diced
1 heaping tblsp snipped fresh chives
You will also need some large squares of muslin or cheesecloth

Line a large sieve with 2 layers of muslin or cheesecloth and place over a bowl.
Blend the tomatoes and salt together for the tomato water in a blender or processor until well chopped.
Pour the tomato pulp into the sieve, cover, and leave for 8 hours in the fridge so that the liquid drips through into the bowl. Do not force the pulp.
Remove the tomato pulp and reserve it for another dish. Season the remaining liquid with pepper and salt if it needs it.
Put the tomato for the gazpacho vegetable garnish into a bowl, cover with boiling water, and leave for 10 seconds. Plunge the tomato into cold water, then peel, quarter, and discard the seeds.
Dice the flesh finely and mix it with the cucumber, pepper, avocado, and chives.
Mix the vegetables and chives into the clear tomato water, divide among glasses, and serve chilled.

Advance preparation: Make the tomato water 2 days ahead and dice the cucumber and pepper 1 day before; cover and chill. Prepare the avocado and chives to order.
Freezing: Not suitable.

right Clear gazpacho

Berry frappé

This deep burgundy colored frappé is a good way of using up any leftover soft berries that you have. Use the best that's in season, substituting blackberries, loganberries, or strawberries if necessary. MAKES 10

8 cups mixed berries, such as black currants, red currants & raspberries
4 cups ice cubes
3½ cups sugar syrup
1¼ cups fresh lime juice
5 cups cold water

Put the berries on a tray lined with plastic wrap. Freeze uncovered for 1½–2 hours, or until the berries are frozen solid.
Divide the frozen berries and ice into 4 batches. Put the first batch into a blender or processor and pulse 5–6 times or until evenly crushed.
Add a quarter of the sugar syrup, lime juice, and water and blend briefly, just enough to combine everything.
Pour into a jug. Repeat with the remaining batches and serve immediately.

Advance preparation: Not suitable.
Freezing: Freeze the berries up to 4 weeks before and cover.

Strawberries & cream frappé

Crushed berries and cream over ice — of all the frappés, this is my favorite. MAKES 10

12 cups strawberries, hulled and halved
4 cups ice cubes
3½ cups sugar syrup
5 cups half-and-half

Put the strawberries on a tray lined with plastic wrap and freeze uncovered for 2 hours or until they are frozen solid.
Divide the frozen strawberries and ice into 4 batches and put the first batch in a blender or processor. Pulse about 5 or 6 times or until evenly crushed.
Pour in a quarter of the sugar syrup and cream. Quickly blend for a few seconds just to incorporate the ingredients.

Pour the frappé mixture into a pitcher and repeat with the remaining batches. Serve immediately, in glasses.

Advance preparation: Not suitable.
Freezing: Freeze the strawberries up to 4 weeks before and cover.

Watermelon frappé

Adding sugar syrup to this frappé enhances watermelon's elusive taste. MAKES 10

4 cups ice cubes
14 cups chopped seeded watermelon flesh
2¼ cups sugar syrup

Put a quarter of the ice cubes into a food processor and pulse until crushed.
Add a quarter of the melon and the sugar syrup and pulse 2–3 times so that the melon is smooth but the ice retains a crushed texture.
Pour the mixture into a pitcher. Repeat with the remaining batches and serve immediately in glasses.

Advance preparation: Cut the melon, cover, and chill up to 4 hours ahead.
Freezing: Not suitable.

Clockwise from top right Strawberries & cream frappé, Berry frappé & Watermelon frappé

Coconut cooler

As this coconut drink isn't overly sweet it's a good cooling accompaniment to hot, spicy Thai and Indian curries. Sometimes I use plain yogurt instead of milk and cream, to make it into more of an Indian lassi-style drink. MAKES 10

5 cups coconut milk
3½ cups milk
1¼ cups half-and-half
3½ cups fresh coconut flesh,
    brown skin removed
1¼ cups sugar syrup
Ice cubes for serving
10 small pieces fresh coconut flesh
    to decorate

Divide all of the ingredients, except for the ice and the pieces of coconut for decorating, into 4 batches.
Blend each batch in a blender or processor for about 1 minute or until the mixture is completely smooth.
Pour over ice in glasses and decorate with the coconut flesh. Serve.

Advance preparation: Make the cooler up to 6 hours ahead, cover, and chill. Add ice to order.
Freezing: Make and freeze the cooler up to 2 weeks before.

Kiwi cooler

Packed with vitamins C and E, not only do kiwifruit make healthy drinks, but their vivid color speckled with fine black seeds makes them an attractive addition to any drinks tray. MAKES 10

2½ lb kiwifruit, peeled and quartered
    + 10 unpeeled quarters to decorate
3½ cups cold water
2½ cups sugar syrup
1¼ cups fresh lemon juice
Ice cubes for serving

Divide the peeled kiwifruit, water, sugar syrup, and lemon juice into 4 batches and then blend each batch in a blender or processor for about 45 seconds or until smooth.

Pour over ice in glasses and decorate with the remaining kiwifruit. Serve.

Advance preparation: Make the cooler up to 6 hours ahead, cover, and chill. Add ice to order.
Freezing: Make and freeze the cooler up to 2 weeks before.

Mango & passion fruit cooler

Really ripe mangoes and passion fruit are essential for this particular cooler. Don't even think about making it unless they are both ripe. The best passion fruit are slightly wrinkled, with an intensely flavored deep orange pulp, while the most succulent variety of mango has sunset colors of red and orange. If ripe mangoes are hard to come by, Indian and Asian shops also sell the excellent Alfonso variety in cans. MAKES 10

5 large mangoes (to yield 6 cups purée),
  peeled and cut from the pit
10 passion fruit + 5 passion fruit,
  halved, to decorate
2¼ cups sugar syrup
2¼ cups fresh lime juice
Ice cubes for serving

Blend the mangoes in a blender or processor until smooth, then pass through a sieve.
Seed and juice 10 of the passion fruit and combine in a pitcher with the mango purée, sugar syrup, and lime juice.
Pour the mixture over ice in glasses. Decorate each glass with a passion fruit half and serve.

Advance preparation: Make the cooler up to 6 hours ahead, cover, and chill. Add ice to order.
Freezing: Make and freeze the cooler up to 2 weeks before.

Left to right Kiwi cooler,
Mango & passion fruit cooler,
Coconut cooler

Breakfast in a glass
Great for Sunday brunches, but also for breakfast on the run. MAKES 10

5 cups pink grapefruit juice or blood
orange juice
5 cups plain low-fat yogurt
½ cup + 2 tblsp clear honey
½ cup + 2 tblsp wheatgerm
Ice cubes for serving

Blend everything, except for the ice, together in a blender or processor. Pour over ice and serve.

Advance preparation: Make up to 8 hours ahead, cover, and chill.
Freezing: Not suitable.

Spiced apple & cinnamon warmer
Serve this on wintry nights at the start of a party or just before everybody departs. Dark rum or Calvados can be added. MAKES 10

One 4-inch piece fresh ginger,
  thinly sliced
4 star anise pods
12 cloves
2 cinnamon sticks
8 cups unsweetened apple juice
¼ cup honey
¼ cup fresh lemon juice
*You will also need a small piece of muslin
or cheesecloth and a piece of string*

Tie the ginger and spices in the muslin or cheesecloth.
Place the spice bag and the rest of the ingredients in a saucepan and heat gently for 30 minutes without boiling.
Remove from the heat and discard the spice bag. Pour the drink into glasses, placing a teaspoon in each to prevent cracking. Serve piping hot.

Advance preparation: Make, cover, and chill up to 1 week ahead. Reheat and pour into a thermos up to 2 hours before serving.
Freezing: Make and freeze up to 2 weeks in advance.

Champagne & sorbet fizzes

This is a grown-up version of an ice cream soda. MAKES 10

1½ cups sorbet, such as black currant, melon, peach, raspberry, or strawberry
2 bottles champagne or other sparkling white wine
You will also need an ice cream scoop

Make 10 small balls from the sorbet. Transfer to a tray, cover, and freeze.
Chill the champagne glasses.
Place a scoop of sorbet in the bottom of each glass and slowly fill with champagne. Serve immediately.

Advance preparation: Chill the glasses.
Freezing: Scoop the sorbets and freeze up to 3 days before.

Poinsettias

A lovely champagne cocktail to serve at autumn cocktail parties. MAKES 10

2 cups cranberry juice
5 oz Cointreau or Grand Marnier liqueur
2 bottles champagne or other sparkling white wine

Mix the cranberry juice and liqueur together and divide among glasses. Top with champagne and serve immediately.

Advance preparation: Mix the juice and liqueur up to 4 hours before, cover, and chill. Top up with champagne to order.
Freezing: Not suitable.

Whisky sours

Fresh lemon juice is vital to give this drink its distinctive sour flavor. MAKES 10

2¼ cups Scotch whisky
1¼ cups fresh lemon juice
⅓ cup sugar syrup
3 egg whites

Divide the ingredients into batches. Pour each batch into a cocktail shaker and shake briefly. Pour into glasses and serve.

Advance preparation: Squeeze the lemons 2 hours before, cover, and chill.
Freezing: Not suitable.

Mojitos

This Cuban rum punch is a variation of the original daiquiri, made famous by Ernest Hemingway. Top up with soda water for a more refreshing drink. MAKES 10

3½ cups light rum
1¼ cups fresh lime juice
⅓ cup sugar syrup
Ice cubes for serving
Wedges of lime for decoration
Sprigs of mint for decoration
Soda water (optional)

Stir the rum, lime juice, and sugar syrup together. Divide the ice among glasses, pour over the rum mixture, decorate with the lime wedges and mint, and serve.

Advance preparation: Mix the rum, lime juice and syrup up to 4 hours ahead, cover, and chill. Pour over ice to order.
Freezing: Not suitable.

Long Island iced tea

A misnomer if ever there was one — the color of this drink is its only similarity to tea! Serve with lots of ice. MAKES 10

3½ oz rum
3½ oz gin
3½ oz vodka
3½ oz tequila
3½ oz Cointreau
7 oz lime juice
1¼ liters Coca-Cola
Ice cubes for serving

Mix the spirits and the lime juice together, then divide between glasses half-filled with ice. Top up with Coke, stir, and serve.

Advance preparation: Mix the spirits and lime juice together up to 4 hours ahead, cover, and chill. Top up with ice and cola to order.
Freezing: Not suitable.

Morgans

Adding sloe gin to this cocktail gives it a deliciously intriguing flavor. MAKES 10

6 cups pink grapefuit juice
1¼ cups sloe gin
1¼ cups dry sherry
1¼ cups Cointreau or Grand Marnier
3 tblsp crème de cassis
Ice cubes for serving

Mix all the ingredients together, pour over ice, and serve.

Advance preparation: Mix everything together, except the ice, up to 4 hours ahead; cover and chill. Add ice to order.
Freezing: Not suitable.

Mint juleps

It's essential to the success of this bourbon cocktail that you crush the mint leaves and sugar together to release the fragrance of the mint. MAKES 10

50 mint leaves
3 tblsp superfine sugar
3 tblsp water
2¼ cups bourbon whiskey
Crushed ice to serve
Sprigs of mint for decoration

Put the mint, sugar, and water together in a small jug. Crush the mint with the back of a spoon until the sugar has bruised the mint and dissolved.
Add the bourbon and mix well. Pour into glasses, top up with crushed ice, and stir.
Decorate each glass with a sprig of mint and serve immediately.

Advance preparation: Not suitable.
Freezing: Not suitable.

right Mint julep

Oyster shooters

If you like oysters, then this is the drink for you! Serve well chilled in small glasses and knock them back in one. MAKES 10

10 small fresh oysters
1¼ cup Clamato juice, chilled
5 oz ice-cold vodka
Freshly ground pepper to taste
½ small cucumber, finely diced

Put an oyster in the bottom of each glass.
Mix the Clamato juice, vodka, pepper, and cucumber together and pour over the oysters. Serve immediately.

Advance preparation: Dice the cucumber 1 day ahead, cover, and chill. *Freezing: Put the bottle of vodka in the freezer up to 8 hours before to chill.*

Chocolate martinis

Purists won't approve of this martini. Not only have I added Cointreau, but it's also served in a chocolate-dipped glass. However, it's a fun party drink. A kumquat can substitute nicely for the twist of orange zest if you prefer. MAKES 10

2½ oz semisweet chocolate, chopped
10 oz ice-cold vodka or gin
15 oz dry vermouth, chilled
5 oz Cointreau, chilled
10 twists of orange zest or 10 kumquats
to decorate

Melt the chocolate in a bowl over a pan of simmering water for 7–10 minutes or until melted.
Pour the chocolate onto a dinner plate, up-end the martini glasses, and dip the rims into the chocolate. Gently shake to remove any excess, stand them upright, and let harden.
Stir the vodka, vermouth, and Cointreau together. Pour into the chocolate-rimmed glasses and add the twist of orange zest or a kumquat. Serve icy cold.

left Simply red

Advance preparation: Prepare the orange zest up to 2 hours before and wrap in plastic wrap.
Freezing: Mix the vodka, vermouth, and Cointreau together; cover and freeze up to 1 day ahead.

Simply red

This bright red cocktail of fruit juices with vodka, grenadine, and bitters is equally delicious without any alcohol. MAKES 10

2½ cups cranberry juice
2½ cups blood orange or ruby orange juice
5 tsp grenadine
Angostura or other bitters to taste
10 oz vodka
Ice cubes for serving

Mix the juices together with the grenadine and bitters to taste. Add the vodka and pour over ice in glasses. Serve.

Advance preparation: Mix all the ingredients together, except the ice, up to 4 hours before; cover and chill.
Freezing: Not suitable.

Gold vodka

This is best drunk icy cold. Give the bottle a good shake before pouring so that the gold is held in suspension, and serve the vodka with caviar-based canapés. Edible gold leaf is available from art shops. MAKES 10

1 pint (570 ml) vodka
4 sheets 23.5- or 24-carat gold leaf

Pour the vodka into a blender. Lift the sheets of gold leaf off the backing paper with the tip of a knife and add to the vodka. Blend for 30 seconds.
Transfer the vodka back to the bottle and put in the freezer for 2 hours to chill.
Shake the bottle before serving and pour the vodka into small glasses.

Advance preparation: See below.
Freezing: Freeze the gold vodka up to 4 weeks before.

Negronis

Count Camillo Negroni, a citizen of Florence in the 1920s, gave his name to this bitter Italian cocktail. MAKES 10

10 oz Campari
10 oz gin
10 oz sweet vermouth
Ice cubes for serving

Mix all the ingredients together and pour over ice in glasses. Serve.

Advance preparation: Mix up to 4 hours ahead, cover, and chill. Pour over ice to order.
Freezing: Not suitable.

Hot buttered rum

Let your guests add their own spiced butter to this warming drink and use cinnamon sticks instead of spoons to stir. MAKES 10

2¼ cups dark rum
2¼ cups boiling water
10 cinnamon sticks
for the spiced butter
4 tblsp unsalted butter, softened
¼ cup packed brown sugar
½ tsp ground cinnamon
½ tsp ground nutmeg
½ vanilla bean, split & the seeds scraped out, or ¼ tsp vanilla extract

Beat together all the ingredients for the spiced butter with a wooden spoon until creamy. Transfer to a serving bowl.
Heat the rum in a pan until very hot but not boiling, then add the boiling water.
Put a spoon in each glass to prevent it cracking, then pour in the rum mixture. Remove the spoons and add the cinnamon sticks.
Serve with the butter, allowing about 1 heaped teaspoon per glass. Stir well.

Advance preparation: Mix the hot rum and boiling water together 2 hours before and put into a thermos.
Freezing: Make the spiced butter up to 4 weeks ahead and freeze.

New Orleans coffee with chocolate spoons

Coffee spoons are dipped into melted chocolate for a frivolous touch. MAKES 10

for the spoons
2 oz semisweet chocolate, chopped
for the New Orleans coffee
2¼ cups strong hot coffee
1 tsp ground cinnamon
1 tblsp sugar
Pared zest of 2 oranges
Pared zest of 1 lemon
4 oz brandy
4 oz Cointreau or Grand Marnier
You will also need some muslin or cheesecloth and 10 coffee spoons

Melt the chocolate in a bowl over a pan of simmering water for about 10 minutes.
Dip the spoons in the chocolate and put them on a plate. Chill for 45 minutes.
Remove the chocolate spoons from the fridge 10 minutes before serving.
Heat the coffee, cinnamon, sugar, and both zests over low heat in a pan. When hot but not boiling, stir in the alcohol.
Strain the coffee through muslin or cheesecloth and serve in cups with the chocolate spoons.

Advance preparation: Dip the spoons up to 4 days ahead, cover, and chill. Make the coffee up to 2 hours ahead, cool, then gently reheat for 10 minutes until hot.
Freezing: Not suitable.

New Orleans coffee with chocolate spoons

Index

The first number given is the page on which the recipe appears.

Cook's notes

● Use measuring spoons for accuracy. All spoon measures are level unless otherwise stated.

● All vegetables are peeled unless otherwise stated.

● All eggs are large unless otherwise stated.

● All garlic cloves, vegetables, and fruit are medium sized unless otherwise stated.

● It may seem that in some of the advance preparation instructions it is not worth spending time preparing tiny amounts of food ahead of time. However, if you are making these recipes for large numbers, it is worthwhile.

● The elderly, children, pregnant women, and those suffering from immune deficiency diseases should avoid eating raw or lightly cooked eggs due to the potential risk of salmonella.

● If you are unsure whether any of your guests are allergic to peanuts or peanut oil, always use olive oil or canola oil rather than oils labeled groundnut, peanut, or vegetable.

Acknowledgments

There are so many people involved in the production of a book, and this one is no exception.

I would particularly like to thank Lindsey Greensted-Benech, our wonderful head cook at Lorna Wing Ltd. for fourteen years, who did all the testing and cooking of the recipes for this book and prepared the food for photography. She deserves accolades for her patience, skill, and dedication.

Thank you to the team who helped produce the book: Jan Baldwin for her impeccable eye and stunning photography; Peter Dixon, Jan's able assistant; and Sue Parker, whose superb styling enhanced our food enormously. At Conran Octopus, thanks go to Jenni Muir, for her constant encouragement and patience in editing the text and recipes; Leslie Harrington for her skill and expertise in art-directing the book so beautifully; and Mary Staples, the art editor, for implementing the design.

Maryse Boxer at Chez Joseph was generous in lending some of her fabulous collection of tableware for photography. Thanks also to Sophie Grigson, for generously allowing me to use her mother's recipe; Paula Pryke for the use of her flat for shooting; and to my literary agents, Felicity Rubinstein and Sarah Lutyens.

Martine de Gues gave practical advice, while my partner Brian McCombie put up with having no social life and lots of leftovers for months on end. Chris Wing, my sister, deserves special thanks, as she kept our catering business going in my long absence and made sure that everything continued to run smoothly. Thanks also go to the others at the company — Maria Radcliffe, Jonathan Attwood, Sue Hargreaves, and Ged Deutrom — who took good care of all our clients while I was away.

There have been many people over the years who have supported and inspired me, and I would like to thank them too. Early on in my career, Lady Elizabeth Anson of Party Planners gave me many wonderful opportunities to cook for some fascinating clients. Both Jasper Conran and his father, Terence, had an enormous impact on my cooking education and taught me so much about good food. Delia Smith and Michael Wynn Jones gave me my first opportunity to write, and without them I would not have felt able to undertake this book.

Finally, there was my mother, Lottie, who encouraged me in the kitchen from a very early age, and my father, Richard, who uncomplainingly ate all the dreadful childish results. Thank you.